Study Guide

Economic Issues and Policy

THIRD EDITION

Jacqueline Murray Brux

University of Wisconsin, River Falls

THOMSON

SOUTH-WESTERN

Australia · Canada · Mexico · Singapore · Spain · United Kingdom · United States

THOMSON

SOUTH-WESTERN

Study Guide for

Economic Issues and Policy, 3/e

Jacqueline Murray Brux

VP/Editorial Director:
Jack W. Calhoun

VP/Editor-in-Chief:
Mike Roche

Publisher of Economics:
Michael B. Mercier

Acquisitions Editor:
Peter Adams

Developmental Editor:
Sarah K. Dorger

Marketing Manager:
Lisa L. Lysne

Production Editor:
Cliff Kallemeyn

Technology Project Editor:
Peggy Buskey

Media Editor:
Pam Wallace

Manufacturing Coordinator:
Sandee Milewski

Design Project Manager:
Tippy McIntosh

Production House/Compositor:
DPS Associates

Printer:
West

For permission to use material from this text or product, submit a request online at http://www.thomsonrights.com.

For more information
contact South-Western,
5191 Natorp Boulevard,
Mason, Ohio 45040.
Or you can visit our Internet site at:
http://www.swlearning.com

CONTENTS

Introduction to Economics

PURPOSE

My purpose in writing this chapter is to introduce you to economics without being too technical. Some of the students who enroll in my Economics of Social Issues course for freshmen never take another economics course. A surprising number, however, discover that economics is relevant, interesting, and worth taking further, more technical courses. We have gained many majors and minors in economics through this course.

Chapter One contains the two concepts that are going to be used throughout the book. It is really important that you become comfortable with the concepts of production possibilities and with supply and demand early on in the course. These concepts will appear over and over throughout the course.

LEARNING OBJECTIVES

The learning objectives for this chapter are:

1. to acquaint you with the ideas of limited resources, opportunity cost, and the need for choice.

2. to enable you to understand basic economic terminology.

3. to help you learn to use the production possibilities model to analyze opportunity costs, unemployment, and economic growth.

4. to enable you to understand the supply and demand model and how markets allocate resources.

5. to introduce you to the concepts of equity and efficiency, market failures, free markets vs. government intervention, micro and macroeconomics, and some of the policy issues that economists study.

STUDY SUGGESTIONS

- As you follow up on your instructor's lectures, be sure to review your notes on a daily basis. This allows you to absorb the information, and you can ask questions in class the next day if you don't understand something. It is *not* a good idea to wait until the night before your exam to start studying this material!

- As you read the textbook, be sure you understand each vocabulary word presented in the margins. Use each one in a sentence.

- Redraw the graphs in the chapter. This will help you make sure you understand the material and help you remember it for a test. Often, the material will look clear in your notes, but until you practice your graphs you may not remember them on your exams. Be sure you understand why curves shift in a particular way.

- Be sure you understand the difference between negative and positive relationships among variables.

- When working with supply and demand graphs and analyzing how a change in some factor affects price and the quantity, *first shift the appropriate curve*, and then see how price and quantity in the new equilibrium compare with price and quantity in the old equilibrium. Be sure to always shift the curve of the group (consumers or producers) that is affected most directly and immediately by the change. Normally you will be shifting only one curve.

- Draw a supply and demand graph and show how a change in each of the factors in Figure 1-16 would shift one of the curves. Be sure to remember that an increase in either demand or supply is a forward shift. (Hint: Think in terms of output increasing along the quantity axis.) *After* you have shifted the curve, look at the resulting changes in price and quantity in Figure 1-17.

- Be sure you understand the difference between a movement along the demand or supply curve (due to a change in the price of a product) and a shift in the entire demand or supply curve (due to a change in some factor *other than* a change in the price of the product.

- Don't check the answers to the following exercises until you have finished them. Then correct any errors. Be sure you understand *why* your answers are incorrect!

- For the multiple-choice and true-and-false questions, see if drawing graphs in the margins helps you to answer the question correctly. (Hint: Do this on exams also.)

- Be sure to take advantage of the features of this textbook that make it easier for you to succeed in the class. These include chapter "roadmaps," economic "toolboxes," the index and glossary, economic applications, summaries, and "questions for discussion." The "questions for discussion" include many web sites that will be useful to you. Also be sure to carefully read the "Viewpoint" sections, which are an important feature of this book and will help you decide whether or not you are a liberal or a conservative in terms of the economic issue at hand. These textbook features are described more carefully in the "Preface to the Student" in the textbook.

Work the following exercises and do the self-test at the end of this section. If you miss a question on the self-test, be sure you understand why you missed it.

PRACTICE EXERCISES

1. In the space below, graph the following production possibilities alternatives. Then answer the following questions.

Alternative	Motorcycles	Robots
A	500	0
B	375	10
C	250	20
D	125	30
E	0	40

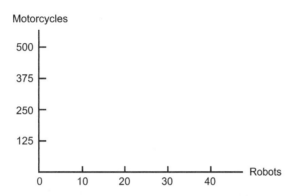

a. What assumptions underlie the production possibilities curve you have drawn?

b. What is the opportunity cost of the first 10 robots? _____ of the last 10 robots? _____

c. Add point M below your production possibilities curve. What does point M represent? _____

d. Can we say which alternative along the curve is best for society? Why, or why not?

e. Can we reach a point outside your production possibilities curve at the present time? _____ Explain.

f. What factors do you think might cause your production possibilities curve to shift outward?

g. Is it possible to shift the production possibilities curve inward? _____ Explain.

2. A production possibilities curve is shown below.

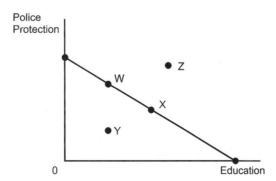

    a.   What does each point on the curve represent?

    b.   What can you say about point Y? _____ about point Z? _____

3. The production possibilities curves for Country A and Country B are shown below. The alternative combinations of capital goods and consumer goods that each country chooses to produce are labeled x and y. Which country would you expect to have the largest growth in the future? _____ Show this on the graphs and explain.

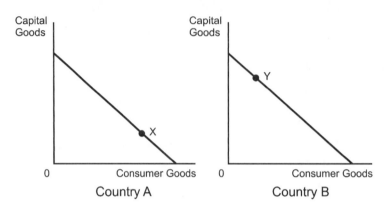

Country A   Country B

4. The supply and demand schedules for steak are shown below. Graph the supply and demand curves and clearly mark the equilibrium price and quantity. Then answer the following questions.

Price (per lb.)	Quantity Supplied	Quantity Demanded
$6	9,000	1,000
5	7,000	3,000
4	5,000	5,000
3	3,000	7,000

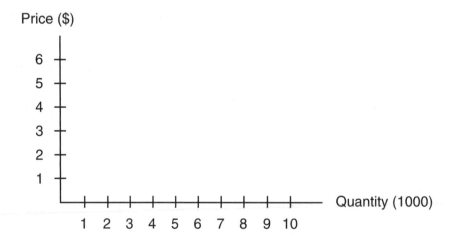

    a.   What is the equilibrium price _____ and quantity? _____
    b.   If price were $6, what would be the result? _____
        If price were $3? _____

In questions 5 through 9, first label your initial equilibrium quantity (Q) along the quantity axis and your initial equilibrium price (P) along the price axis. Then decide which group (producers or consumers) is affected most immediately and directly as a result of the change that is occurring. Then shift the *single* corresponding curve (demand or supply) forward (if it increases) or backward (if it decreases). Finally, label the new quantity (Q´) along the quantity axis and the new price (P´) along the price axis and answer whether those have increased or decreased. Do not answer these latter questions until you have gone through all of the other steps first, because now you can simply read your answers (increase or decrease) off the graph (otherwise you will think in circles and get the wrong answers.) Always follow those steps in order when dealing with a shift in a demand or supply curve.

5. The demand and supply curves for chocolate ice cream are shown below. What shift would you expect if consumer incomes rise? _____ Show this on the graph. What will be the effect on equilibrium price _____ and equilibrium quantity? _____

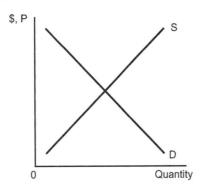

6. Consider the market for crackers below. Assuming that consumers eat soup and crackers together, draw the shift that will occur if the price of soup increases. What will be the effect on the price of crackers? _____ on the quantity of crackers bought and sold? _____ (Hint: Keep in mind that this graph is for the *cracker market*, not the soup market!)

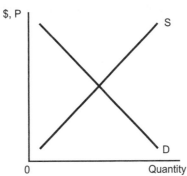

7. Consider the market for shoes below. Draw the shift that will occur if there is an increase in wage rates that increase the labor costs of producing shoes. What will be the effect on the price of shoes? _____ on the quantity of shoes bought and sold? _____

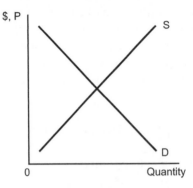

8. Draw the shift that will occur in the market for cranberries below if exceptionally good weather results in a bumper (very large) crop of cranberries. What will be the effect on the price of cranberries? _____ on the equilibrium quantity of cranberries? _____

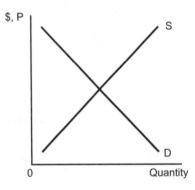

9. Draw the shift that will occur in the market for barley if technological change makes it cheaper and easier to produce barley. What will be the effect on the price of barley? _____ on the equilibrium quantity exchanged? _____

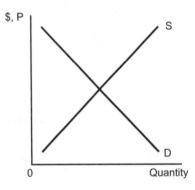

SELF-TEST

Multiple-Choice Questions

1. Which of the following statements are true?
   a. Price and quantity demanded are positively related.
   b. Price and quantity supplied are negatively related.
   c. Buyers are willing and able to buy larger amounts of a product at lower prices than at higher prices.
   d. Sellers are willing and able to sell larger amounts of a product at lower prices than at higher prices.

2. If broccoli and green beans are substitutes, what will be the effect of a decrease in the price of green beans on the market for broccoli? Hint: Keep in mind that we are looking at the broccoli market and not the bean market. Think through the steps: a decrease in the price of green beans ⟶ people to buy more green beans ⟶ demand for broccoli decreases. (Draw a graph in the margins if this is helpful!)
   a. The supply of broccoli will increase.
   b. The demand for broccoli will increase.   = The demand for beans will increase
   c. The supply of broccoli will decrease.
   d. The demand for broccoli will decrease.

Questions 3 and 4 refer to the following graph.

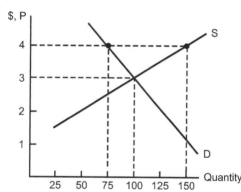

3. What are the equilibrium price and quantity?
   a. $3, 100   b. $4, 150   c. $4, 75   d. $2, 75

4. At what price will there be a surplus of 75 units?
   a. $2   b. $3   c. $4   d. none of the above.

5. If the wheat market initially is in equilibrium, and the price of the fuel needed to harvest the wheat crop increases:
   a. the demand for wheat will increase.
   b. the supply of wheat will decrease.
   c. the supply of wheat will increase.
   d. the demand for wheat will decrease.

6. In terms of the production possibilities curve, economic growth can be shown by a:
    a. movement from a point inside the curve to a point on the curve.
    b. movement upward along the curve.
    c. shift of the curve outward.
    d. movement downward along the curve.

The next two questions refer to the following production possibilities schedule for computers and food.

Alternative	Computers	Food
A	5	0
B	4	10
C	3	20
D	2	30
E	1	40
F	0	50

7. If the economy is currently producing at alternative C, the opportunity cost of one more computer is:
    a. 10 units of food we give up.
    b. 4 units of food we gain.
    c. 3 computers.
    d. cannot say because we don't know the price of computers.

8. The output combination of 2 computers and 20 units of food:
    a. is a better combination than 4 computers and 10 units of food.
    b. results from inefficiency or unemployment of the economy's resources.
    c. would be too expensive for the economy to produce.
    d. would not be attainable without economic growth.

9. The fact that we have limited resources relative to our unlimited wants means that we have:
    a. externalities.
    b. scarcity.
    c. public goods and services.
    d. inefficiency.

10. What do market power, public goods, and spillover costs and benefits have in common?
    a. They are all market failures that keep the private market from resulting in an optimum outcome.
    b. They all imply that the private market will always achieve an efficient outcome.
    c. They all denote situations in which government action in the economy is undesirable.
    d. They are all situations in which the private market is much more efficient than government action.

11. If the demand for broccoli increases:
    a. both equilibrium price and quantity will increase.
    b. both equilibrium price and quantity will decrease.
    c. equilibrium price will increase, but equilibrium quantity will decrease.
    d. equilibrium price will decrease, but equilibrium quantity will increase.

12. If the government taxes the sale of gasoline, it will:
    a. increase the supply of gasoline.
    b. decrease the supply of gasoline.
    c. decrease the demand for gasoline.
    d. increase the demand for gasoline.

13. The best alternative forgone is the definition of:
    a. production possibilities.
    b. scarcity.
    c. opportunity cost.
    d. externality.

14. When we say "all other things equal (constant)" with regard to demand and supply, we meant that:
    a. nothing other than price ever affects demand and supply.
    b. factors other than the price of the product that could affect demand or supply do not change.
    c. the market is not in equilibrium.
    d. there is neither a surplus nor a shortage in the market.

True-and-False Questions

1. All other things equal, price and quantity demanded are negatively related.

2. All other things equal, price and quantity supplied are negatively related.

3. Every point on the production possibilities curve represents full employment of the economy's resources.

4. Public goods and services are generally not provided by free markets in sufficient quantities unless the government intervenes.

5. A good example of a public good is the manufacturing of automobiles.

6. Two of the factors that cause economic growth are technological change and improvements in the quality of resources.

7. Economic growth can be represented by an inward shift of the production possibilities curve.

8. If seller's opportunity costs increase, supply will shift forward.

9. If supply decreases (shifts backwards), both price and quantity exchanged will decrease.

10. If consumer incomes decrease, the demand for most goods will decrease.

11. Pollution and education are examples of spillovers.

12. Market power is the ability to influence market price.

13. High unemployment or inflation means instability in the economy.

14.   Microeconomics deals with the economy as a whole.

ANSWERS TO PRACTICE EXERCISES

1. a. fixed technology and resources and full-employment and efficiency, b. 125 motorcycles, 125 motorcycles, c. unemployment or inefficiency, d. no, depends on society's values, e. no, production possibilities curve shows maximum amounts, f. technological change and increased or improved resource supply, g. loss of resources due to environmental destruction, depreciation of capital, war, or natural disasters.

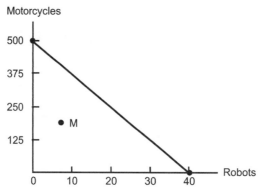

2. a. maximum amounts of education and police protection that can be produced with given technology and resources, b. Y represents unemployment or inefficiency, Z is not attainable in the current time period.

3. A, currently producing more capital goods will shift curve outward over time.

4. a. P = $4, Q = 5,000, b. surplus of 8,000, shortage of 4,000.

5. increase demand, increase price, increase quantity.

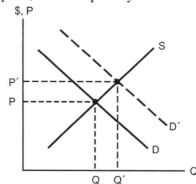

6. decrease demand, decrease price, decrease quantity. (Hint: Write out the process that is occurring here: An increase in the price of soup ➔ people buy less soup ➔ demand for crackers decreases)

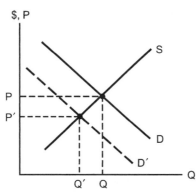

7. decrease supply, increase price, decrease quantity.

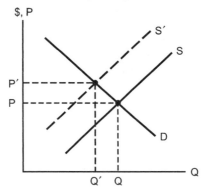

8. increase supply, decrease price, increase quantity.

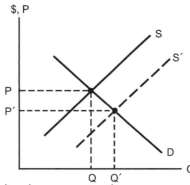

9. increase supply, decrease price, increase quantity.

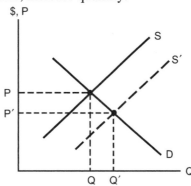

ANSWERS TO SELF-TEST

Multiple-Choice: 1c, 2d, 3a, 4c, 5b, 6c, 7a, 8b, 9b, 10a, 11a, 12b, 13c, 14b
True-and-False: 1T, 2F, 3T, 4T, 5F, 6T, 7F, 8F, 9F, 10T, 11T, 12T, 13T, 14F

2

Crime and Drugs

PURPOSE

In this chapter we look at the controversy over the legalization of drugs, as well as crime and crime prevention. We examine the idea of a public good. Be sure you understand how a public good differs from private goods and how crime prevention is a public good. Also, be sure you understand that cost-benefit analysis is the appropriate tool that economists use to evaluate the effectiveness of any particular type of crime prevention activity.

LEARNING OBJECTIVES

The learning objectives for this chapter are:

1. to help you to recognize a public good.

2. to acquaint you with cost-benefit analysis as a means of evaluating public policy.

3. to enable you to understand the economic argument for legalizing "victimless crimes."

4. to enable you to understand the economic argument against legalizing "victimless crimes."

5. to illustrate the conservative and liberal viewpoints on crime and its prevention.

STUDY SUGGESTIONS

-   As you did in the previous chapter, be sure that you understand each vocabulary word and can use it in a sentence.

-   Again, sit down and redraw the graphs. Do you understand why the supply and demand curves shift as they do? Understanding the reasons for the shifts is essential for understanding the material.

• Do you understand why an addict's demand curve for drugs would be steeper (more inelastic) than a casual user's demand curve? Be sure you understand how this will affect usage (equilibrium quantity) if the supply of drugs increases.

• This issue of crime clearly illustrates the difference between the conservative and liberal viewpoints in social matters and in economics. Be sure you understand the distinction.

Work the following exercises and do the self-test at the end of this section. If you miss a question on the self-test, be sure you understand why you missed it.

PRACTICE EXERCISES

1. Assume that in 1970 the U.S. was at point A on the production possibilities curve below. Indicate its present position on the graph (you need to show only the direction of the change). What does this new position reflect?

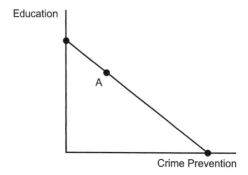

2. The following exercise has to do with the effects of legalizing drugs, or any so-called victimless crime.

    a. The curve below shows the demand for illegal drugs. What, if anything, would happen to this demand if drugs were legalized? _____ Show in the graph.

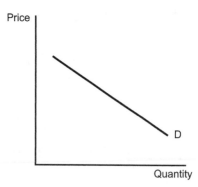

List reasons for any shift of the curve:

b. The supply curve for illegal drugs is shown below. What, if anything, would you expect to happen to this supply if drugs were legalized? _____ Show in the graph.

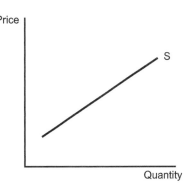

List reasons for any shift of the curve:

c. The graph below shows both the supply and demand for illegal drugs. Show the expected changes from legalization on the graph by shifting both curves appropriately. Can you predict what would happen to price? _____ to equilibrium quantity (usage)? _____

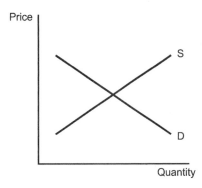

3. In the space below draw the demand curves of (a) drug addicts and (b) casual drug users. Which is more inelastic?

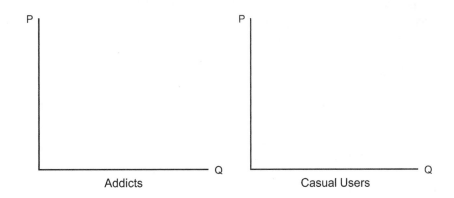

4. List the three characteristics of public goods and explain why these characteristics make public goods different from other goods.

5. What are some of the benefits of crime prevention activities?, and the costs? Are all costs and benefits easy to measure?

6. Write a paragraph comparing the liberal and conservative economic viewpoints on the legalization of drugs. Then compare the economic viewpoints with the positions of social liberals and conservatives.

SELF-TEST

Multiple-Choice Questions

1. When we say that one of the characteristics of a public good is nonexcludability, we mean that:
    a. one person using the good does not adversely affect others' use of the good.
    b. since people who do not pay for the good cannot be kept from benefiting from the good, some of them will be free riders.
    c. the good cannot be divided into small enough pieces to be sold on the private market.
    d. all of the above.

2. The biggest percentage increase in expenditures on the U.S. criminal justice system in the past twenty-five years is in the area of:
    a. police protection.
    b. the judicial system.
    c. corrections.
    d. drug interdiction.

3. Legalizing marijuana would lead to a(n):
    a.   increase in demand and supply.
    b.   decrease in demand and supply.
    c.   decrease in demand and increase in supply.
    d.   increase in demand and decrease in supply.

4. Which of the following is sometimes considered a victimless crime?
    a.   prostitution.
    b.   theft.
    c.   rape.
    d.   arson.

5. A "victimless crime" is one that:
    a.   hurts property, not people.
    b.   is the result of a transaction to which both parties mutually consent.
    c.   no one can be found to bring charges.
    d.   is done by accident.

6. Recently funding was continued for the popular Project DARE drug education program, although studies indicate that the program is not effective in keeping young people off drugs. It is likely that:
    a.   Project DARE's costs outweigh its benefits.
    b.   the program will be discontinued immediately.
    c.   the program will be improved.
    d.   all of the above.

7. A benefit of taxing the sale of legalized drugs is that:
    a.   demand would decrease and so would price.
    b.   supply would decrease and so would usage.
    c.   price would decrease due to a decrease in supply.
    d.   price would decrease despite an increase in demand.

8. If we were to regulate legalized drugs by taxing them, and we knew that drug A was much more harmful than drug B:
    a.   we would tax them both the same.
    b.   we would tax drug B more highly than drug A.
    c.   we would tax drug A more highly than drug B.
    d.   we would avoid taxing either drug.

9. Some people argue that the War on Drugs' efforts to prevent drugs from entering the U.S. from other countries have been ineffective because:
    a.   whenever supply from one area of the world is disrupted, supply from other areas increase.
    b.   in some countries, peasants cannot easily shift to other, equally profitable, legal crops.
    c.   in some countries, drug cartels have more power than the government.
    d.   all of the above.

10. On the production possibilities curve below, the movement from point A to point B implies that:

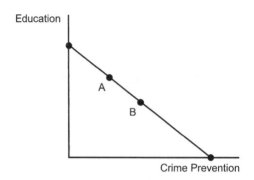

    a.   we now use less of our resources for crime prevention and more for education.
    b.   we now use less of our resources for education and more for crime prevention.
    c.   we are now less efficient at providing education.
    d.   we are now less efficient at crime prevention.

True-and-False Questions

1. Pornography is often considered a victimless crime.

2. If the supply of marijuana increases due to its legalization, usage will increase more if the demand for marijuana is inelastic than if it is elastic.

3. U.S. expenditures on the judicial system have increased more rapidly than expenditures on corrections.

4. If we legalize drugs, usage will decrease, all other things equal.

5. The "risk premium" from drugs' illegality causes supply to decrease.

6. Both liberal and conservative economists strongly support the legalization of drugs.

7. More government anti-drug expenditures are for demand-side programs than for supply-restriction programs.

8. When we say that public goods are nonrivalrous, we mean that one person using them does not interfere with another person's use.

9. On the issue of the legalization of drugs, social conservatives and economic conservatives hold the same viewpoint.

10. The government manages to stop at least sixty percent of illegal drugs entering the United States from other countries.

ANSWERS TO PRACTICE EXERCISES

1. movement along the curve to the right means we are producing more crime prevention relative to education.

2   a. increase, the demand curve shifts forward, people who do not try drugs solely because they are illegal would try them
    b. increase, costs would go down because the risk premium of operating in an illegal market would be eliminated so the supply curve would shift forward
    c. price might increase or decrease, but usage would certainly increase

3. addicts have more inelastic demand curves (represented by a steeper demand curve).

4. indivisibility—cannot be divided into units easily sold on the private market
    nonrivalrous—one person's benefiting from it doesn't keep others from also benefiting.
    nonexcludable—cannot keep people who don't pay from benefiting from the public goods so there will be freeriders
    Private goods are divisible into salable units, rivalrous so that one person's use keeps others from benefiting from the good, and excludable, so that people who do not pay for them can be prevented from using them.

5. benefits: crimes prevented, safer streets, better business since shoppers aren't afraid, etc.
    costs: budgets of police, courts and prisons, curtailment of civil liberties, etc.

6. Economic conservatives are more likely to favor drug legalization, whereas economic liberals are more likely to oppose legalization. The situation is the opposite for social conservatives and social liberals.

ANSWERS TO SELF-TEST

Multiple-Choice: 1b, 2c, 3a, 4a, 5b, 6a, 7b, 8c, 9d, 10b
True-and-False: 1T, 2F, 3F, 4F, 5T, 6F, 7F, 8T, 9F, 10F

3

The Environment

PURPOSE

The purpose of this chapter is to convince you that pollution and the environment are indeed economic issues, and to explain how economics enters into decisions to pollute as well as solutions to the pollution problem.

LEARNING OBJECTIVES

The learning objectives for this chapter are:

1. to raise your consciousness (if it has not already been raised) of environmental problems and your own role in causing and preventing these problems.

2. to introduce you to the concept of externalities, particularly negative ones, and how they result in inequity associated with spillover costs and benefits and inefficiency associated with misallocation of resources.

3. to acquaint you with an economic way of analyzing pollution as a by-product of production (and consumption), as well as policy designed to reduce pollution caused by industry (and consumers).

4. to enable you to recognize the appropriate level of government to be involved in pollution control decisions.

5. to introduce you to the concept of marginal cost as it relates to the cost of reducing pollution by one additional unit.

6. to encourage you to think about pollution on the national as well as the international level.

7. to introduce you to the methods used to regulate the environment.

8. to discuss with you the incentives used to encourage recycling and conservation.

9. to help you determine whether you are liberal or conservative (or middle of the road) when it comes to environmental issues.

STUDY SUGGESTIONS

- Be sure you understand each vocabulary word. Be able to use each one in a sentence.

- Redraw the graphs in the chapter. Be sure you understand why curves shift in a particular way and how price and quantity change when a curve shifts.

- Be sure you understand the meaning of the vertical distance between the two supply curves in the case of pollution and in the case of an emissions or effluent fee.

- Do not be confused about the concept of the social supply curve. Costs of production, in one form or another, are always reflected in supply curves. The *private* supply curve reflects all of the costs of production that fall upon the producer in the production of a product. It does not reflect the pollution costs, however, since these are not borne by the producer (unless the government imposes a tax on the polluting firms). The *social* supply curve reflects all of the *social* costs of production, that is, all of the costs that fall upon society as a whole. This includes the pollution cost borne by society, *and also includes* the private costs of production borne by the firms (since they too are part of society).

- The idea of a "socially optimum" amount of a good or service is a difficult concept, since it is so theoretical. We really cannot measure all of the social costs of pollution, much less *one additional unit* of pollution control. We have to imagine it though. Think of a unit as one pound of pollutants in a stream, for example.

- The concept of marginal cost is introduced in this chapter, in the context of costs of pollution control. Marginal simply means change. It asks the question: what will be the *additional* cost of one *additional* unit of pollution control? Note the emphasis on the word 'additional'.

- We don't expect marginal cost to remain constant. In particular, we expect that as each successive unit of pollution control is achieved, it costs more and more to achieve it. In other words, it is fairly cheap (and easy) to achieve the first unit of pollution control. It is much more expensive (and difficult) to achieve the hundredth unit of pollution control. That is all we mean by rising marginal cost!

- Read through the material on marketable pollution permits carefully. It is a little complicated, but a very interesting idea. Try to understand how it works through incentives and results in least-cost pollution reduction.

- Don't be confused about the word "subsidy". Society often uses the word loosely, where in this chapter we have a specific idea in mind. A subsidy is simply the opposite of a tax. Just as a tax placed on the producer increases the costs of production, we can think of a subsidy as reducing these costs. Therefore we can think of a subsidy as shifting the supply curve forward, instead of back. *And always remember,* a forward shift of supply is an increase, while a backward shift of supply is a decrease!

- Be sure to think about the international dimensions of environmental issues. You can probably think of many more international examples that are not listed in the text.

- Think about whether you are liberal or conservative when it comes to environmental issues. Make sure that you understand and can explain why!

Work the following exercises and do the self-test at the end of this section. If you miss a question on the self-test, be sure you understand why you missed it.

PRACTICE EXERCISES

1. Consider a hypothetical market for pharmaceuticals in a small country, assuming that the production of pharmaceuticals causes pollution of near-by streams and lakes. S_p represents the private market supply curve, while S_s is the social supply curve. S_s reflects the full social costs of production.

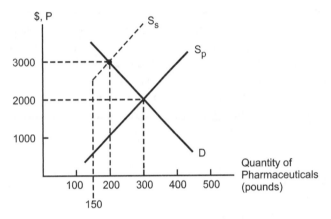

   a. Specifically, what costs are reflected in the social supply curve?

   b. What is represented by the vertical distance between the two supply curves? What amount is this?

   c. Why is it possible that production of less than 150 pounds of pharmaceuticals results in no spillover costs?

   d. What is the equilibrium quantity of pharmaceuticals produced in the private market? _____ What is the socially optimal quantity of pharmaceuticals? _____ Why do we say that the private market results in an overallocation of resources to pharmaceutical production? _____ Why is this a problem? _____

2. Consider a hypothetical market for chemicals and a hypothetical market for tomatoes, assuming that the chemical producing companies create polluted run-off. Also, assume for the sake of simplicity that the demand curve and the private supply curve in each market are identical. Draw the shift in the chemical industry that occurs when chemical producers decide it is too expensive to clean up the run-off and they allow it to flow down the ravines instead. Draw the shift in the tomato market as farmers are forced to purify or otherwise divert the water before it damages their tomato crops.

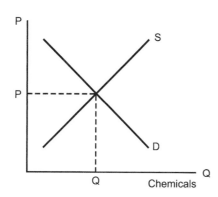

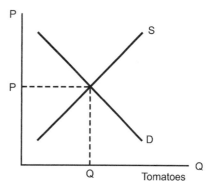

a. What will be the effect of the decision on the equilibrium quantity _____ and price _____ of chemicals?

b. What will be the effect on the equilibrium quantity _____ and price _____ of tomatoes?

c. What is the effect on the allocation of resources in both the chemical _____ and tomato _____ markets?

(Note that this is a real situation of pollution that of the author observed in Mexico. The government eventually told the farmers that they could no longer produce food because of the contamination, and that they should produce flowers instead. The farmers told the author that people only buy flowers on Valentine's Day, and now they no longer receive an adequate income for their labors.)

3. Consider a hypothetical market for dishwashers, assuming that pollution is caused by the production of dishwashers. The supply curve shown is the private market supply curve. Draw the shift that will occur if the government imposes an emissions fee on the polluting firms. What effect will this have on the price paid by consumers? _____ Is it appropriate that consumers of dishwashers pay a higher price? Why?

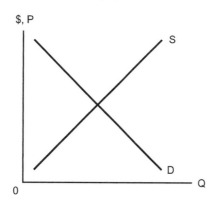

SELF-TEST

Multiple-Choice Questions

1. Pollution is defined as:
   a. litter.
   b. waste that is not recycled.
   c. anything that is toxic.
   d. anything that is discarded.

2. Which of the following is true?
   a. Externalities can be either costs or benefits.
   b. Externalities never result from consumption activities.
   c. Education produces spillover costs onto society.
   d. Pollution never affects markets in which the pollution does not occur.

3. The social costs of production are equal to:
   a. the pollution costs borne by society.
   b. the private costs of production borne by the producer.
   c. both the pollution costs and the private costs of production.
   d. none of the above.

4. When production of a product creates pollution, we know that the private decision making of a firm (without government intervention) will result in:
   a. equity.
   b. efficiency.
   c. overallocation of resources to this industry.
   d. underallocation of resources to this industry.

5. The earliest efforts to control pollution in the U.S. through legislation came from:
   a. city governments.
   b. state governments.
   c. the federal government.
   d. international organizations.

6. Effluent fees are taxes on production that causes:
   a. water pollution.
   b. air pollution.
   c. land pollution.
   d. any type of pollution.

7. The use of pollution permits results in the purchase of the permits by:
   a. the firms for whom the costs of reducing pollution are the highest.
   b. the firms that have the least amount of pollution.
   c. the firms that have the highest marginal costs of pollution control.
   d. all of the above.

8. A $2 charge per bag for the collection of garbage should result in:
    a. an incentive for consumers to reduce garbage.
    b. an incentive for consumers to buy products with less packaging.
    c. an incentive for consumers to recycle or compost.
    d. all of the above.

9. An industry that causes pollution results in:
    a. an overallocation of resources to this industry.
    b. inequity for society.
    c. inefficiency.
    d. all of the above.

10. A tax on gasoline:
    a. increases the price paid by consumers for gasoline.
    b. reduces the supply of gasoline.
    c. results in less gasoline use.
    d. all of the above.

True-and-False Questions

1. Pollution causes a misallocation of resources.

2. Liberals are more likely to accept the federal government role in environmental regulation than are conservatives.

3. Externalities may include costs or benefits that are shifted from the private market onto society.

4. City governments are almost always the appropriate level of government to make decisions about pollution control.

5. "Technology forcing" refers to the setting of standards that force firms to use specific technologies to control pollution.

6. Rising marginal costs of pollution control mean that it costs less to remove an additional unit of pollution when pollution levels are high than when pollution levels are low.

7. "Standards" are more likely to result in least-cost pollution control than the use of emission and effluent fees.

8. Conservatives are more likely to favor pollution control policies that utilize market forces, such as pollution fees.

9. The installation of catalytic converters on automobiles is an example of a "design standard."

10. Environmental quality is a luxury good.

11. A "performance standard" specifies a certain level of performance or compliance that must be met.

ANSWERS TO PRACTICE EXERCISES

1. a. private costs plus spillover (pollution) costs, b. the spillover (pollution) cost that is equal to $2,000, c. the natural cleansing properties of our environment, d. 300, 200, we produce more than we would desire if pollution costs were considered, it is a problem of scarcity of productive resources (since scarce resources are overallocated to one product, resources will be underallocated to another product).

2. a. increase, decrease, b. decrease, increase, c. overallocation, underallocation

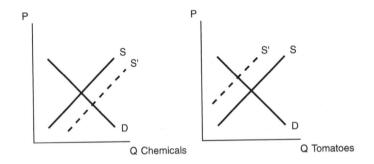

3. decrease supply; increase; yes, because they indirectly cause pollution when they buy this product

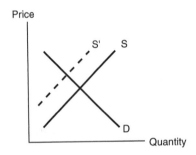

ANSWERS TO SELF-TEST

Multiple-Choice: 1b, 2a, 3c, 4c, 5a, 6a, 7d, 8d, 9d, 10d
True-and-False: 1T, 2T, 3T, 4F, 5T, 6T, 7F, 8T, 9T, 10T, 11T

4

Education

PURPOSE

In this chapter we analyze American education. This chapter is, of course, relevant to you, the student. First we look at public elementary and secondary (K–12) education and the inequality created by the property-tax financing it. Then we look at the differences in expenditures and revenue sources for public and private colleges. Finally we look at some current issues in higher education, such as decreased state funding for public university systems. In all of this, we are concerned with equal educational opportunity.

LEARNING OBJECTIVES

The learning objectives for this chapter are:

1. to have you think about education's spillover benefits to society.

2. to illustrate the effects of education's spillover benefits on resource allocation and equity.

3. to acquaint you with the effects of property tax financing of K–12 education.

4. to consider the differences in public spending on education between the United States and many other industrialized countries.

5. to discuss the quality of K–12 education and possible policies to improve it.

6. to analyze the different sources of revenues and expenditures of private and public colleges.

7. to help you to analyze the effects of subsidies to education such as state tax appropriations, student loans, and Pell grants.

8. to discuss with you the effects of investment in human capital with regard to college education.

9. to inform you about the national trend of decreasing state support for public university systems.

10. to delineate the conservative and liberal viewpoints on education, including the use of vouchers, affirmative action, and the "No Child Left Behind" policy.

STUDY SUGGESTIONS

- Be sure you understand each vocabulary word. Use each one in a sentence.

- Redraw the graphs in the chapter. Be sure you understand why curves shift in a particular way.

- What is your opportunity cost to attend your school? See if you can figure out all the direct and indirect costs of your education. Then fit them into the investment in human capital graph in the text.

- Talk to your instructors or your college placement office about the salaries of jobs in your major. What is the range? What could you expect as a starting salary and as a salary after you have acquired some work experience? See if you can estimate the increased lifetime earnings from your college education. Fit that into the investment in human capital graph in the text. Do you consider your education a good investment?

- Think about the pros and cons of vouchers, affirmative action, and "No Child Left Behind." Be able to argue "for" and "against" in each case.

Work the following practice exercises and take the self-test. If you miss a question on the self-test, be sure you understand why.

PRACTICE EXERCISES

1. Jeremiah attends Metro U. He pays $8,000 per year in tuition. His books cost $2,000 each year. Fees are $600 per year. Jeremiah works part-time while he is in school and earns $6,000. The job he quit to go to school paid $16,000 per year. What are the total opportunity costs of a year of school for Jeremiah? _____

2. Jenny's estimated earnings without a college degree and with a college degree are shown below. If she goes to college, she will not work during the years she is 19-22 years of age. The direct costs of attending State U to earn a degree total $60,000 over the years she plans to attend.

Age	Annual Earnings Without Degree	Annual Earnings With Degree
19-22	$10,000	
23-30	16,000	$23,000
31-40	19,500	30,000
41-50	22,000	35,000
51-65	23,500	42,000

a. What are Jenny's indirect costs of attending State U? _____

b. What are Jenny's increased earnings (ages 23-65) from attending college? _____

c. Should Jenny attend? _____

3. City X has a property tax base of $200,000 per student. City Y has a property tax base of $400,000 per student.

    a. If they are both going to spend $2,000 per student on K–12 education, what must each of their property tax rates be? _____

    b. If they each set a tax rate of 1 percent, how much will they spend per student? _____

4. The supply and demand graph below is for higher education provided through the private market. It does not show the spillover benefits of education to society. Show spillover benefits by shifting the appropriate curve and then tell how the existence of spillover benefits means that the market allocates resources inefficiently.

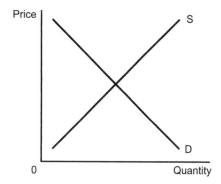

SELF-TEST

Multiple-Choice Questions

1. Because education has spillover benefits for society, the private market will:
   a. overallocate resources to education.
   b. produce too much education.
   c. underallocate resources to education.
   d. produce the optimum amount of education for society.

2. Property tax financing of public elementary and secondary education results in:
   a. equal educational opportunity because school is free to the student and the student's family.
   b. more educational spending per student in wealthy school districts than in poor districts.
   c. equal spending per student in all school districts.
   d. inner city schools receiving more tax revenues per student than suburban schools.

3. The theory of investment in human capital implies that:
    a. slavery is an inefficient economic system.
    b. students make decisions to invest in productivity-increasing education in much the same way that businesses make investment decisions.
    c. private schools are more efficient than public schools.
    d. public schools are more efficient than private schools.

Answer the next three questions on the basis of the following graph:

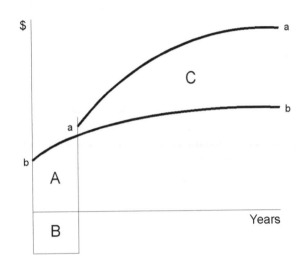

4. The increase in lifetime earnings due to education is shown by:
    a. C   b. A
    c. aa   d. B

5. The indirect costs of education are shown by:
    a. C   b. A
    c. aa   d. B

6. The direct costs of education are shown by:
    a. C   b. A
    c. bb   d. B

7. The largest subsidy to higher education is:
    a. guaranteed student loans.
    b. state tax appropriations for public university systems.
    c. Pell grants.
    d. scholarships.

8. State tax appropriations to public university systems benefit:
    a. lower-income students more than high-income students.
    b. all income classes the same, because all students receive the same subsidy.
    c. middle-and higher-income students more than low-income students.
    d. only 25 percent of students, since most students go to private colleges.

9. The principal source of revenues for private colleges is:
    a. endowment income.
    b. federal subsidies.
    c. tuition.
    d. state tax subsidies.

10. It may be becoming more difficult for very low income students to afford college because:
    a. the maximum Pell grant pays a smaller percent of college expenses than it used to.
    b. none of the financial aid packages available recompense students for the opportunity cost of forgone wages.
    c. tuition accounts for a larger share of the expenses of our public university systems than previously.
    d. all of the above.

11. Which of the following would supposedly increase competition among schools?
    a. charters
    b. magnets
    c. vouchers
    d. all of the above

True-and-False Questions

1. The largest subsidy to college students is the state tax appropriations to public university systems.

2. Tax appropriations to public universities have increased as a percentage of state budgets as the number of high school graduates has increased in the last 15 years.

3. Public universities spend only half as much as private universities on instruction.

4. Inner city schools are generally funded at a higher level (per student) than suburban schools.

5. School segregation no longer exists in the United States.

6. Tuition vouchers would allow students to choose to go to either a public or private school (assuming they could afford it).

7. Conservatives support tuition vouchers and magnet schools because they supposedly increase competition in education.

8. Liberals oppose tuition vouchers because they would reduce finances to already troubled public inner city schools.

9. Proposals to charge different college tuition for different majors are based on the idea that the different tuition levels would increase the efficiency of universities' internal allocation of resources.

10. Since student aid is available, all young people in the United States have an equal opportunity to obtain a college education.

11. The total direct public expenditures on education as a share of gross domestic product is highest in the United States in comparison with other industrialized countries.

12. The Supreme Court recently ruled that vouchers are constitutional.

13. The largest source of funding for public institutions of higher education is state governments.

14. The largest source of funding for private institutions of higher education is state governments.

ANSWERS TO PRACTICE EXERCISES

1. Direct costs = $8,000 + $2,000 + $600 = $10,600,
   indirect costs = $16,000 – $6,000 = $10,000,
   total = $20,600

2. a. 4 years earnings at $10,000 per year = $40,000 (Forgone earnings age 19–22)
   b.   23–30:   8 years at $7,000 $ 56,000
        31–40:   10 years at $10,500   105,000
        41–50:   10 years at $13,000   130,000
        51–65:   15 years at $18,500   277,500
                                             $568,500
   c. yes, total cost = $60,000 + $40,000 compared to the increased earnings in part b.

3. a. 2,000/200,000 = 1%, 2,000/400,000 = 0.5%
   b. $2,000 for X, $4,000 for Y

4. With spillover benefits, D is larger and equilibrium quantity is greater. The existence of spillover benefits means that the private market underallocates resources to education.

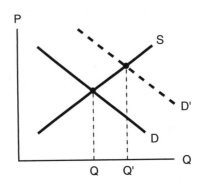

ANSWERS TO SELF-TEST

Multiple-Choice: 1c, 2b, 3b, 4a, 5b, 6d, 7b, 8c, 9c, 10d, 11d
True-and-False: 1T, 2F, 3F, 4F, 5F, 6T, 7T, 8T, 9T, 10F, 11F, 12T, 13T, 14F

5

Discrimination

PURPOSE

This is the first chapter among the three chapters focused specifically on the issue of equity. The purpose is to look at discrimination against minorities in the United States We define minority from a sociological perspective as a group with less access to positions of power and prestige in society. Thus women are included as a minority. We look at Census Bureau statistics, consider the most common theories (or explanations) about discrimination, discuss the difficulty in actually measuring the extent of discrimination, and finally look at government policy toward discrimination. Recall that the term "equity" means fairness. While we all may agree that discrimination is unfair, we may certainly disagree about the ways to reduce the problem.

LEARNING OBJECTIVES

The learning objectives for this chapter are:

1. to acquaint you with the changing racial and ethnic composition of the United States.

2. to define the term *minority* from its sociological perspective.

3. to delineate the dimensions of labor market discrimination.

4. to introduce you to some of the more common explanations for the existence of discrimination.

5. to acquaint you with the costs of discrimination to individuals and to society.

6. to help you understand the role of government intervention in labor markets by means of legislation and affirmative action.

7. to discuss with you other types of discrimination and policies aimed at these types of discrimination.

8. to help you to understand the conservative and the liberal viewpoints on discrimination and government policy toward discrimination.

STUDY SUGGESTIONS

- Students often come to my class under the assumption that labor market discrimination no longer exists and that policies to reduce discrimination are unnecessary. They are often surprised to see the earnings differentials between men and women and between whites and other minorities. Young women are especially shocked to see that upon graduation, they are likely to receive much smaller earnings than young men with similar educations. Come to the class with an open mind, and be prepared to discuss controversial issues such as affirmative action in an open and respectful manner.

- Students are often confused about unemployment rates, and believe (as do most Americans) that unemployment rates are higher for women than men because many women choose to stay home with their young children. You must realize that a person is considered unemployed *only* if he or she is seeking but unable to find a job outside of the home. This will be discussed in detail in Chapter 14, but you should be aware of it now.

- Pay attention to some of the precise meanings used by economists. For example, the differences between "earnings" and "income," and between "mean" and "median" are important. Similarly, we look at the earnings of full-time workers in order to remove the effect of part-time workers (who are more likely to be women) on earnings differentials.

Work on the following exercises and take the self-test at the end of this section. If you miss a question on the self-test, be sure you understand why you missed it.

PRACTICE EXERCISES

1. Assume that there are 54,000 workers in a hypothetical labor force (other than professors) at your university or college. Half of them are men, and half are women. There are three occupations that they can pursue: custodian, groundskeeper, or program assistant. Assume that due to tradition or other reasons, custodian and groundskeeper are male jobs and program assistant is a female job. The demand is the same in all three occupations, and the demand schedule for any of the occupations is shown below. Draw the graph of demand for all three occupations, with the quantity of labor on the horizontal axis and the wage rate on the vertical axis.

Wage Rate	Workers Demanded
$12	4,500
11	9,000
10	13,500
9	18,000
8	22,500
7	27,000
6	31,500
5	37,000

a. With the occupational segregation described above, what will be the equilibrium employment and wage rate in each occupation? _____ What is the women's wage? _____ What is the men's wage? _____

b. Now assume that occupational segregation ends, so that either men or women can randomly work in any of the three occupations. What will be the equilibrium employment in each occupation? _____ What is the women's wage? _____ What is the men's wage? _____

2. Answer the following questions about each of the explanations for labor market discrimination discussed in the chapter.

a. Does the employer discriminate because he/she is prejudiced in an emotional sense?
Statistical Discrimination _____
Occupational Segregation _____

b. Is the discriminating employer at a cost disadvantage?
Statistical Discrimination _____
Occupational Segregation _____

c. Is it reasonable to expect that discrimination of this type will be eliminated by market forces?
Statistical Discrimination _____
Occupational Segregation _____

3. With reference to the tables of data in the chapter, answer the following.

a. What percent of the median weekly earnings of a full-time male worker are the median weekly earnings of a full-time female worker? _____

b. What percent of the median weekly earnings of a full-time white male worker are the median weekly earnings of a full-time black male worker? _____ a Hispanic male worker? _____

c. The median annual earnings of full-time, year-round male workers with master's degrees is what percent of the median annual earnings of full-time, year-round female workers with master's degrees? _____

d. The median annual earnings of full-time, year-round white workers with bachelor's degrees is what percent of the median annual earnings of full-time black workers with the same level of education? _____

e. The 2002 female unemployment rate was _____ whereas the male unemployment rate was _____. The black unemployment rate was _____ while the white unemployment rate was _____.

SELF-TEST

Multiple-Choice Questions

1. "Our nation is moving toward two societies, one black, one white—separate and unequal" is a quotation from:
    a. President George W. Bush in his first State of the Union Address.
    b. President George H. W. Bush on the first Martin Luther King day.
    c. The Kerner Commission in 1968.
    d. The Reverend Martin Luther King ten days prior to his assassination.

2. According to the text, the major economic cost to society of discrimination is:
    a. social unrest and occasional riots.
    b. the unhappiness of those who are discriminated against.
    c. inefficiency that results in less national output than could be produced with society's resources.
    d. tokenism.

3. Occupational crowding results in:
    a. lower wages for the groups that are crowded into relatively few occupations.
    b. higher wages for the groups that have access to more occupations.
    c. decreased national output.
    d. all of the above.

4. The most troublesome problem in measuring discrimination is that:
    a. it is difficult to isolate the effects of discrimination, culture, and individual choice.
    b. data on wages are not available.
    c. data on employment are not available.
    d. eliminating discrimination would decrease national output.

5. Wage discrimination means that:
    a. more productive workers are paid higher wages than less productive workers.
    b. a male lawyer will make more than a female retail clerk.
    c. a minority worker is paid a lower wage than a non-minority worker in the same job, although they are equally productive.
    d. workers with rare skills and abilities earn higher wages than unskilled workers.

6. Discrimination in human capital occurs when:
    a. certain groups have higher high school dropout rates than others.
    b. more resources are invested in education and training for some groups than others so some groups receive better education than others.
    c. minorities are the last hired and the first fired.
    d. certain groups find it difficult to enter some occupations.

7. Employment discrimination may show up in unemployment statistics because:
    a. women have much higher unemployment rates than men.
    b. African Americans and Hispanics have unemployment rates that are approximately twice the white unemployment rate.
    c. reverse discrimination occurs and minorities are hired instead of white males.
    d. affirmative action results in women being hired instead of men.

8. The elimination of racial and gender discrimination would:
    a. increase the nation's gross domestic product.
    b. put the United States at a disadvantage in international trade.
    c. result in higher wages for white males.
    d. decrease efficiency in our labor markets.

9. Statistical discrimination:
    a. occurs when employers screen workers by looking at the characteristics of the worker's group instead of individual worker characteristics.
    b. can actually decrease the costs of the discriminator if there are significant differences between employee groups.
    c. results in the employer missing outstanding workers of the group discriminated against.
    d. all of the above.

10. Liberals are more likely than conservatives to:
    a. believe that affirmative action is necessary to eliminate discrimination.
    b. believe that discrimination will disappear without government intervention in the economy.
    c. believe that discriminators are at such a significant cost disadvantage in comparison to nondiscriminators that they will eventually either stop discriminating or leave the market.
    d. oppose affirmative action programs to eliminate the different pay scales for men's and women's jobs.

True-and-False Questions

1. Women are more numerous than men, and therefore women cannot be considered a minority.

2. There is considerable occupational segregation on the basis of gender in the United States.

3. The Civil Rights Act of 1964 established the Equal Employment Opportunity Commission.

4. Men and women have approximately the same rates of unemployment.

5. If we adjust for level of education, most differences in the incomes of fully employed men and women are eliminated.

6. According to statistics in the text, our nation is becoming more diverse.

7. Racial and ethnic minorities have significantly higher unemployment rates than whites.

8. Free public education through the twelfth grade eliminates discrimination in human capital.

9. Paying different wage rates to employees is always discriminatory.

10. The Civil Rights Act of 1964 made discrimination on the basis of gender and race illegal.

ANSWERS TO PRACTICE EXERCISES

1. a. 13,500 (half of the) men employed as custodians and 13,500 (the other half of) men as groundskeepers at a wage rate of $10; 27,000 (all) women employed as program assistants at a wage rate of $7; women's wage = $7, men's wage = $10; b. 18,000 (one third of all workers) in each occupation at a wage rate of $9, women's wage = $9, men's wage = $9

2. a. no, no, b. no, no, c. no, no

3. read!

ANSWERS TO SELF TEST

Multiple-Choice: 1c, 2c, 3d, 4a, 5c, 6b, 7b, 8a, 9d, 10a
True-and-False: 1F, 2T, 3T, 4T, 5F, 6T, 7T, 8F, 9F, 10T

6

U. S. Poverty

PURPOSE

The purpose in writing this chapter is to introduce you to the problem of poverty in the United States. Students often think of poverty in the abstract: we have stereotypical images of poor people, but we never think of ourselves or other students as being poor. It is my hope that you will realize that poverty affects a broad array of people, including some of your classmates, and that many of our stereotypes about poverty may be false.

LEARNING OBJECTIVES

The learning objectives for this chapter are:

1. to help you envision the lives of poor people, so that you can better understand their circumstances.

2. to help you understand the concepts of relative poverty, income distribution, money income, income transfers, and in-kind transfers.

3. to encourage you to think about income distribution in the United States, whether it is becoming less equal, and how it compares with other countries.

4. to help you understand the concept of absolute poverty, the official definition of poverty, and the concept of the poverty line.

5. to help you realize that poor people are poor despite any government assistance they receive, and that being poor does not mean that they will necessarily receive any government assistance.

6. to help you think about life at the poverty line, in terms of how much income is available and how this income is spent.

7. to enable you to understand how the poverty rate in the United States has changed over time, who the poor are in the United States, and what groups of people are more likely to be poor.

8. to encourage you to think about the "feminization of poverty."

9. to help you to think about the causes and solutions to poverty, as well as the enormous complexity of the problem of poverty.

10. to assist you in understanding the recent changes in the welfare system.

11. to help you think about whether you are liberal or conservative in terms of poverty issues.

STUDY SUGGESTIONS

- Learn the definitions of the vocabulary words, and be able to use them in a sentence.

- Pay attention to "ball park" numbers for poverty rates and income distributions when these are emphasized in the text, as well as trends in the numbers and comparisons between different groups of people.

- Be sure you understand the concept of "money income." The definition of this term is important when considering whether or not various changes in our economy affect official poverty rates and income distribution.

- Be sure you understand the composition of the poor (that is, who the poor consist of), and the percentage of various groups of people who are poor (that is, which groups of people are more likely to be poor). For example, 68% of the poor people are white, but only about 10% of white people are poor.

- Realize that while everyone seems to know a poor woman who has had additional babies in order to receive additional assistance or a poor father who has sold his food stamps in order to buy cigarettes, these are exceptions to the rule. Be willing to let go of your stereotypes about the poor, unless you can back them up with statistics.

- Make sure you understand the criticisms of the "Aid to Families with Dependent Children (AFDC)" program, and how the "Personal Responsibility and Work Opportunity Reconciliation Act (PRC) is designed to improve on it.

- Make sure you can list the various reasons for poverty and the various solutions to the poverty problem. A complete list will indicate just how complex the poverty problem is.

- Think about whether you are liberal or conservative in terms of the poverty issue.

- Think about the people in your class. Do you think that any of them might be poor? Does this change your feelings towards them? Does this change your feelings about the poor? Be sure that you avoid stereotyping and stigmatizing the poor.

Work through the practice exercises and the self-test. Make sure you understand any questions you may have missed.

PRACTICE EXERCISES

1. (This question is based on the appendix.) Construct a Lorenz curve based on the following income distribution. What is the meaning of the 45° line? _____

Percent of Total Population	Percent of Total Money Income Received
Poorest Fifth	10%
Second Fifth	15%
Third Fifth	20%
Fourth Fifth	25%
Richest Fifth	30%

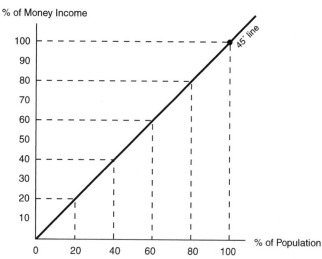

2. (This question is based on the appendix.) Consider the two hypothetical Lorenz curves that follow. Which one represents the greatest equality in income distribution (1st or 2nd)? _____ How can you tell? _____

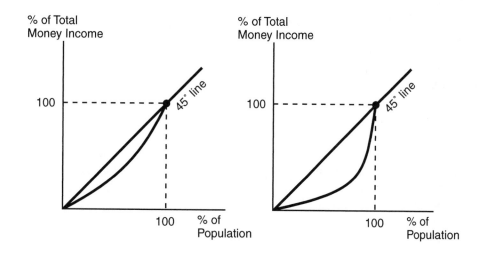

SELF TEST

Multiple-Choice Questions

1. From 1981 to 2002, the richest fifth of the U.S. population has received:
    a. a declining share of total money income in the United States.
    b. an increasing share of total money income in the United States.
    c. a constant share of total money income in the United States.
    d. this is not discussed in the textbook.

2. The Earned Income Credit is actually a form of:
    a. a negative income tax.
    b. a food stamp program.
    b. AFDC.
    c. an in-kind transfer.

3. "Money income":
    a. is calculated before payment of taxes.
    b. includes in-kind transfers.
    c. excludes income transfers.
    d. all of the above.

4. Which of the following was *not* one of the reasons listed in the text for the "feminization of poverty"?
    a. discrimination in the labor market.
    b. domestic violence.
    c. teenage pregnancies.
    d. laziness due to the very high levels of child support (from the absent spouse).

5. Which of the following is an example of an "investment in human capital"?
    a. spending to construct a bridge.
    b. spending to construct a factory.
    c. spending to assure education of people.
    d. all of the above.

6. Which of the following is a universal entitlement in the United States?
    a. public education.
    b. child care.
    c. maternity leaves.
    d. all of the above.

7. Which of the following is *not* true? It had been argued that "Aid to Families with Dependent Children (AFDC)" created incentives for:
    a. families to break up.
    b. women to have additional babies.
    c. people to go to work.
    d. people to migrate to higher-benefit states.

8. A "block grant" is:
    a. a lump of money given by the federal government to state governments.
    b. used by states as they wish to develop programs to meet a broad category of need.
    c. used in a program that replaces the AFDC program.
    d. all of the above.

9. W-2 stands for:
    a. Wisconsin Works.
    b. Wyoming Watches.
    c. Work is Welcome.
    d. Way 2 the future.

10. TANF stands for:
    a. transitional assistance for new fathers.
    b. training and new futures.
    c. temporary aid for needy families.
    d. teaching about nutrition in families.

11. Which of the following is *not* true about welfare under the PRA?
    a. It emphasizes work.
    b. It allows flexible state programs.
    c. It allows most people to stay in the welfare system for their lifetimes.
    d. It involves grants from the federal government to the states.

12. The current (2002) poverty rate is about:
    a. 3%.
    b. 12%.
    c. 23%.
    d. 34%.

13. Relative poverty:
    a. is measured by the income distribution.
    b. refers to people being poor compared to other people.
    c. is measured using the concept of "money income".
    d. all of the above.

14. Which of the following is a social insurance?
    a. Medicaid.
    b. Social Security.
    c. Supplemental Security Income.
    d. All of the above.

True-and-False Questions

1. The richest fifth of the U.S. population receives almost 50% of total money income in the country.

2. Since 1993, the U.S. poverty rate has increased dramatically.

3. The largest number of poor people in the United States is white.

4. Children under age 18 have the highest poverty rate of any age group in the United States.

5. The poverty line for a family of 4 is approximately $40,000.

6. Medicare is the public medical program for low income people.

7. Recession results in fewer job opportunities.

8. The higher-wage manufacturing sector in the United States has grown at the expense of the low-wage service sector.

9. A negative income tax generally has no work incentive built into it.

10. The "Personal Responsibility and Work Opportunity Reconciliation Act (PRA)" eliminated AFDC.

11. From 1994 to 1999, welfare caseloads were cut approximately in half.

12. The earned income credit is only for married working couples with children.

13. Most people who have left welfare for work since the PRA went into effect are now earning very high wages.

14. The 1996 PRA expanded food stamp benefits for legal immigrants.

ANSWERS TO PRACTICE EXERCISES

1. First, determine the *cumulative* percentages of money income going to the fraction of total families.

Percent of Total Population	Percent of Total Money Income Received
Poorest Fifth	10
Poorest Two Fifths	25 (is 10 + 15)
Poorest Threes Fifths	45 (is 10 + 15 + 20)
Poorest Four Fifths	70 (is 10 + 15 + 20 + 25)
Poorest Five Fifths (total families)	100 (is 10 + 15 + 20 + 25 + 30)

Now construct the Lorenz curve with the following coordinates: (0,0), (20,10), (40,25), (60,45), (80,70), (100,100). Smoothly connect the coordinates. The graph is shown on the next page. The resulting Lorenz curve will be bowed out from the 45° line. The 45° line shows all coordinates in the graph where the value on the horizontal axis is equal to the value on the vertical axis. (That is, the 45° line shows perfect equality.)

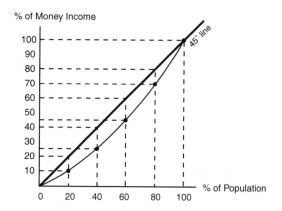

2. The 1st graph shows greater equality in income distribution. Remember this by keeping in mind that a Lorenz curve directly on the 45° line shows perfect equality. The 1st graph has the Lorenz curve closer to the 45° line.

ANSWERS TO SELF-TEST

Multiple-Choice Questions: 1b, 2a, 3a, 4d, 5c, 6d, 7c, 8d, 9a, 10c, 11c, 12b, 13d, 14b
True-and-False Questions: 1T, 2F, 3T, 4T, 5F, 6F, 7T, 8F, 9F, 10T, 11T, 12F, 13F, 14F

7

World Poverty

PURPOSE

The purpose of this chapter is to acquaint you with the less developed countries of the world, as well as the conditions in and needs of these countries. Most importantly, we will consider some policies that might create economic development in these countries, including policies conducted by the United States.

LEARNING OBJECTIVES

The learning objectives for this chapter are:

1. to acquaint you with the less developed countries (LDCs) of the world.

2. to help you understand gross national income (GNI) per capita, the range of GNI per capita in LDCs around the world, and the growth rate of gross domestic product (GDP) per capita in various LDCs.

3. to point out to you the flaws of using GNI and GDP data to measure the well-being of residents of LDCs, including problems relating to the composition of GDP and the distribution of income.

4. to encourage you to think about the real meaning of economic development, insofar as it includes a reduction in poverty, an improvement in standards of living (measured by life expectancies, infant mortality rates, and so on), and economic growth.

5. to assist you in considering many aspects of agricultural development, and human and natural resource development.

6. to help you understand women's roles in development, as well as the issues of population growth and AIDs.

7. to assist you in thinking about urbanization, employment, and rural-urban migration.

8. to help you appreciate the concept of people-oriented economic development that includes attention to women, indigenous people, and the poor.

STUDY SUGGESTIONS

- Be sure you can define all of the vocabulary words, and that all of the definitions make sense to you.

- If your instructor has not provided you with a map of the world, then go find one in the library or on the Internet and run a copy. Every time a country is mentioned in the text, look for it on the map and know what region of the world it is in.

- Think about the reasons for paying particular attention to women in development. Do they make sense to you?

- Our traditional thinking about economic development has often been in terms of urban industrialization, since that is how the United States developed. Does it make more sense to you to focus on rural agricultural development in many LDCs?

- Think about the need for a people-oriented strategy of economic development. Does this make sense to you? Why or why not?

- Be sure you can work through the calculations of economic growth. Realize that economic growth can be positive, negative, or zero.

- Be sure you can work through the graph of a price ceiling. Keep in mind that if a price ceiling is to have an effect on the market, the price ceiling must be *below* the market equilibrium price. Price ceilings are the opposite of price floors, such as the agricultural price supports that will be discussed in Chapter 12. Price ceilings are intended to assist consumers by keeping prices artificially low, whereas price supports are intended to help suppliers by keeping prices artificially high. Note that we *do not* shift any curves in the graph of the price ceiling!

- Think about whether you are liberal or conservative when it comes to economic development. What are some of the policies a person with your view would support?

Work the practice exercises and take the self-test. Be sure you understand why you missed any questions.

PRACTICE EXERCISES

1. Suppose that a poor African country has a GNI equal to $500 million and a population of 5 million people. Calculate the value of GNI per capita. _____

2. Is it possible for a country to have an average annual growth rate of GDP per capita equal to zero? _____ Calculate the 1990–2000 average annual growth rate of GDP per capita for a small Latin American country with an average annual GDP growth rate of 3% and an average annual population growth rate of 3%. _____ Repeat this exercise for an African country with an average annual GDP growth rate of 2% and an average annual population growth rate of 4%. _____

3. Consider the market for millet in the African country of Niger, represented by the following graph. Label the equilibrium price P_0 along the price axis. Now label a price ceiling P_c along the price axis. Label the new quantity demanded Q_D and the quantity supplied Q_s along the quantity axis. What is the problem that results? _____

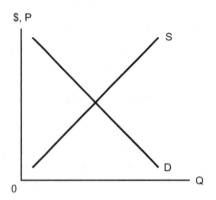

SELF-TEST

Multiple-Choice Questions

1. According to the textbook, what country has the highest GNI per capita?
    a. United States.
    b. Switzerland.
    c. Canada.
    d. Norway.

2. When considering what GDP consists of, we are analyzing:
    a. the distribution of GDP.
    b. the composition of GDP.
    c. the growth of GDP.
    d. the value of total GDP.

3. Singapore and South Korea are classified as:
    a. newly incorporated countries.
    b. agriculturally sound countries.
    c. non-importing countries.
    d. newly industrializing countries.

4. Examples of investment in human capital include:
    a. health care.
    b. education.
    c. training programs.
    d. all of the above.

5. Deforestation contributes to:
    a. soil erosion.
    b. desertification.
    c. declining soil fertility.
    d. all of the above.

6. Economic development results in lower birthrates because:
    a. child survival improves.
    b. agricultural productivity improves.
    c. women have greater income-earning opportunities.
    d. all of the above.

7. Which of the following is *not* an example of informal sector employment?
    a. shoe shining
    b. drug dealing
    c. steel production
    d. sewing clothing

8. Capital-intensive technology is defined as technology that:
    a. utilizes large amounts of capital.
    b. minimizes the use of capital.
    c. produces capital items, such as machinery.
    d. produces capital items, such as food.

9. Which of the following is entailed in the definition of economic development?
    a. reduction in poverty
    b. increase in industrialization
    c. increased rural-urban migration
    d. more capital-intensive technology

10. Costa Rica has a higher life expectancy than the country of Argentina because:
    a. Costa Rica is more prosperous than Argentina.
    b. Costa Rica spends less money on the military than does Argentina.
    c. Costa Rica has a higher GNI per capita than Argentina.
    d. all of the above.

11. A major issue for indigenous people in Chiapas state in Mexico is the right:
    a. to free speech.
    b. against taxation without representation.
    c. to land.
    d. to a jury trial.

12. A legally imposed maximum price for a good or service is a:
    a. price floor.
    b. price support.
    c. price ceiling.
    d. tariff.

13. Informal employment:
    a. consists primarily of service occupations.
    b. exists in unofficial settings.
    c. is often low-wage paying.
    d. all of the above.

14. Agricultural development requires:
    a. market prices for agricultural products.
    b. rural credit programs.
    c. gender analysis.
    d. all of the above.

15. Social overhead refers to:
    a. factories and machinery.
    b. roads and communications.
    c. politics.
    d. family relationships.

True-and-False Questions

1. Investment in human capital is designed to improve the productivity of people.

2. Land distribution is a serious issue in Zimbabwe.

3. Sierra Leone has among the world's lowest life expectancy and the world's highest infant mortality rate.

4. Price ceilings on food products contribute to shortages of food, reduced incentives for food production, and reduced incomes to farmers.

5. Export cropping refers to the pattern of cutting short all production for export.

6. Buffer stocks are often used to create greater instability of agricultural prices.

7. Women are primarily responsible for producing most subsistence food crops in much of the Third World.

8. According to the text, New York City is the world's most populated city.

9. Efforts to improve the urban sector may backfire as large numbers of people move to the cities when city life is improved.

10. Liberal economists are more likely than conservatives to focus on the problems of poverty and unequal income distribution in efforts to achieve economic development.

11. The United States has the world's most unequal income distribution.

12. Labor-intensive technology utilizes large amounts of labor relative to capital.

13. Desertification is the process of turning deserts into irrigated crop land.

14. Subsistence food is grown primarily for export.

15. It is important to improve the agricultural sector in less developed countries because that is generally where most poor people live.

ANSWERS TO PRACTICE EXERCISES

1. $500 million / 5 million = $100

2. Yes, 3% – 3% = 0%, 2% – 4% = – 2%

3. Place a price ceiling somewhere below the market equilibrium price. Then trace the price ceiling over to the demand and supply curves, and label the quantity demanded (Q_D) and quantity supplied (Q_S) as indicated along the quantity axis below. A shortage will result. (Note: You do not shift any curves in this graph!)

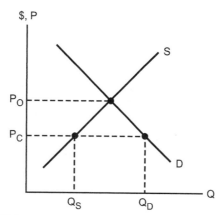

ANSWERS TO SELF-TEST

Multiple-Choice: 1b, 2b, 3d, 4d, 5d, 6d, 7c, 8a, 9a, 10b, 11c, 12c, 13d, 14d, 15b
True-and-False: 1T, 2T, 3T, 4T, 5F, 6F, 7T, 8F, 9T, 10T, 11F, 12T, 13F, 14F, 15T

8

Market Power

PURPOSE

This chapter introduces you to the concept of market power and its abuse. From the very outset, let's make a distinction between a firm's bigness and market power. A firm that is small in absolute size, but lacks competition in the industry, has market power. Conversely, very large firms that face substantial competition have very little market power. You will look at the problem of market power, as well as the factors that lessen market power, and at government policy toward market power.

LEARNING OBJECTIVES

The learning objectives for you in this chapter are:

1. to acquaint you with the concept of market power.

2. to enable you to differentiate between market power and firm size.

3. to clarify the concept of a market.

4. to enable you to understand the measurement of market power by the concentration ratio, as well as some problems involved in measuring market power.

5. to acquaint you with the sources of market power.

6. to acquaint you with the effects of market power.

7. to help you understand the roles of technological change, import competition, and antitrust in lessening market power.

8. to help you understand the use and misuse of economic regulation.

9. to illustrate the conservative and liberal viewpoints toward market power, antitrust, and economic regulation.

STUDY SUGGESTIONS

- As you did in previous chapters, be sure you understand each vocabulary word and can use it in a sentence.

- Sit down and redraw the graphs. Do you understand how a competitive firm cannot by itself cause a shift in the market supply, and therefore cannot influence the market price of its product? Do you understand that the monopoly firm's demand curve *is* the market demand curve because it is the only firm in the market? These are crucial to understanding the rest of the material.

- Keep in mind that market power has extensive implications for prices, output levels, efficiency, and equity. While it may *sound* like a boring topic, it is actually quite important and interesting!

Work the following exercises and do the self-test at the end of this section. If you miss a question on the self-test, be sure you understand why you missed it.

PRACTICE EXERCISES

1. A market demand and supply curves for widgets are shown below. What will be the equilibrium price? _____ the equilibrium quantity? _____

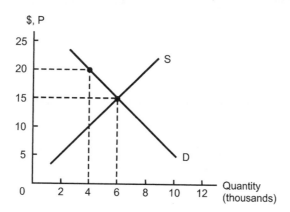

Now assume that one firm becomes a monopoly producer of widgets. That firm decides to increase its price to $20. Explain how it would increase the price.

2. Tell whether the following variables are higher or lower for a monopoly in comparison to a competitive market.

price _____

output _____

profits _____

efficiency _____

3. Suppose there are six firms in the gadget industry, each producing the following percents of total gadget industry output. What is the concentration ratio for the gadget industry?

_____

Firm	Share of Total Output
1	40
2	30
3	15
4	8
5	4
6	3

SELF-TEST

Multiple-Choice Questions

1. A competitive market is characterized by:
   a. many small buyers and sellers.
   b. a standardized product.
   c. no barriers to entry or exit.
   d. all of the above.

2. A competitive firm is a price _____ while a monopoly is a price _____
   a. maker, taker.
   b. taker, maker.
   c. maintainer, cutter.
   d. increaser, maintainer.

3. Which of the following is *unlikely* to have significant market power?
   a. the only dentist in a small, isolated town.
   b. the local newspaper.
   c. a manufacturer of prescription drugs.
   d. a large producer of corn.

4. A monopolist's demand curve is:
   a. the same as the market demand curve.
   b. horizontal.
   c. vertical.
   d. upward sloping.

5. Economies of scale are:
   a. decreasing average costs as output increases.
   b. a barrier to entry into some markets.
   c. the result of the technology used to produce a product.
   d. all of the above.

6. For the U.S. automobile industry, the principal constraint on market power is:
    a. the U.S. antitrust system.
    b. import competition.
    c. rapid technological change in auto design.
    d. Environmental Protection Agency regulation.

7. A monopoly makes greater profits than comparable competitive markets by:
    a. charging a lower price for the same level of output.
    b. producing more output at higher prices.
    c. producing less output in order to get a higher price.
    d. being more efficient than firms in competitive markets.

8. Patents, product differentiation, and occupational licensing are all:
    a. constraints on market power.
    b. barriers to entry.
    c. forces for more effective competition between firms.
    d. present in purely competitive markets.

9. If the three manufacturers of widgets sign an agreement to limit their output and hold the price of widgets above the competitive level, it is:
    a. price fixing.
    b. price leadership.
    c. legal under U.S. antitrust laws.
    d. price discrimination.

10. When manufacturers with market power charge greater markups above cost for repair parts than for their complete products, it is an example of:
    a. cartel.
    b. price fixing.
    c. price discrimination.
    d. price leadership.

True-and-False Questions

1. Because a monopoly has market power, it can produce any output it wants to and charge any price it wants to.

2. Natural monopolies often are granted exclusive franchises by the government and regulated by a government agency.

3. The demand curve of a monopoly is the same as the downward sloping market demand curve.

4. All other things equal, a monopoly produces more output than a comparable competitive market.

5. Because they are larger firms, monopolies are more efficient than competitive firms.

6. Technology is not a factor affecting market power.

7. The U.S. antitrust system is effective in combating both cartels and price leadership.

8. Patents not only encourage invention and innovation, but also act as a barrier to entry into the market.

9. A competitive firm can benefit by setting its own price.

10. The essence of market power is the firm's ability to influence the market price of its product.

ANSWERS TO PRACTICE EXERCISES

1. $15, 6000, decrease quantity to 4,000

2. higher, lower, higher, lower

3. 40 + 30 + 15 + 8 = 93 or 93%

ANSWERS TO SELF-TEST

Multiple-Choice: 1d, 2b, 3d, 4a, 5d, 6b, 7c, 8b, 9a, 10c
True-and-False: 1F, 2T, 3T, 4F, 5F, 6F, 7F, 8T; 9F, 10T

9

International Trade

PURPOSE

The purpose here is to expand your knowledge of international economics. Indeed, this is the second of three international chapters spaced throughout the book—all equally relevant. It is probably the most technical of the three chapters (in terms of graphs and numerical examples), but nevertheless is straightforward and relies only on graphs you have seen before: production possibilities and demand and supply. The focus of attention is international trade, with international finance (specifically exchange rates) discussed in the appendix.

LEARNING OBJECTIVES

The learning objectives for this chapter are:

1. to expand your knowledge of the international economy.

2. to explore with you the controversies over free trade and global capitalism that have culminated in protests, such as the one at the World Trade Organization conference in Seattle in 1999, and subsequent global protests.

3. to help you understand the significance of international trade to the U.S. and the world economies, to realize that trade can be mutually beneficial, and to learn about absolute and comparative advantage.

4. to help you understand the distribution of benefits in the case of free trade, and why some groups oppose free trade and favor trade restrictions.

5. to enhance your interest in the less developed countries (LDCs) of the world, and to help you discover the special problems of LDCs with respect to trade.

6. to assist you in recognizing the interaction between politics and trade in cases such as Iran, Cuba, China, and Vietnam.

7. to help you learn about international trade agreements, and in particular, the North American Free Trade Agreement (NAFTA).

8. to help you develop your own viewpoints on free trade, trade restrictions, and NAFTA.

9. to assist you in understanding exchange rates in the context of flexible exchange rate systems (appendix).

STUDY SUGGESTIONS

- Students are often intimidated by international economics (as is the American public). It may help you to keep in mind the following:

  - ➢ You can understand the benefits of specialization and trade when you think about whether you are better off trying to be self-sufficient versus specializing in a job you are good at and using your income to buy the things you need.

  - ➢ You can understand the concept of comparative advantage by using the production possibilities graph you are already familiar with.

  - ➢ You can understand the effects of free trade and the effects of trade restrictions by using the demand and supply graphs you are already *very* familiar with.

  - ➢ You can also understand how exchange rates are determined by using demand and supply graphs (appendix).

- If you are very careful, you will notice that the examples of comparative advantage and the consumption possibilities curve with trade are not entirely possible, since the country that lacks absolute advantage in both goods is constrained by the amount it can produce of the good in which it has the comparative advantage. (The left end of the consumption possibilities curve would not really be possible.) You may want to think of it as being possible if we extend the time period beyond one year (permitting stockpiling) or if we consider more than two countries. Let's simply resolve this by referring to the consumption possibilities curve as a "theoretical consumption possibilities curve."

- As always, be sure you can define each vocabulary word and be sure that the definition makes sense to you.

- Finally, always redraw the graphs in the text and make sure you understand why a curve shifts a particular way.

Work through the practice exercises and self-test first, and then check your answers. Make sure you understand why you may have missed any questions.

PRACTICE EXERCISES

1. Consider the following table showing that each U.S. worker can produce either 4 refrigerators or 8 bicycles per day, while each Chilean worker can produce either 1 refrigerator or 6 bicycles per day.

Country	Refrigerator Production	Bicycle Production
U.S.	4	8
Chile	1	6

a. Which country has an absolute advantage in refrigerator production? _____

b. Which country has an absolute advantage in bicycle production? _____

c. Which country has a comparative advantage in refrigerator production? _____

d. Which country has a comparative advantage in bicycle production? _____

e. Can it benefit the U.S. to engage in trade with Chile? _____

2. Based on information in the previous question:

a. Draw in the (straight line) production possibilities curve for 1 worker in the United States per day.

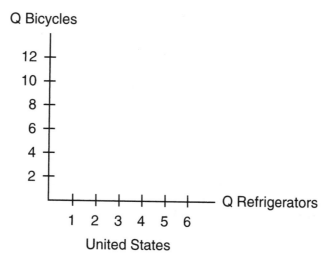

b. Now suppose the U.S. decides to specialize completely in refrigerator production, and trades with Chile at a mutually beneficial trade ratio of 1 refrigerator for 3 bicycles. Draw in the (straight line) U.S. consumption possibilities curve with trade in the previous graph. Is the United States better off with or without trade with Chile? _____ (Keep in mind that you have drawn a "theoretical consumption possibilities curve.")

3. Consider the following graph of the U.S. peanut industry. Domestic (U.S.) demand is represented by the demand curve D, and domestic (U.S.) supply is represented by the supply curve S. Draw the shift that will occur if the United States begins to freely import peanuts from other countries. Label the new free trade price (P_T), and the new quantity demanded (Q_D) by U.S. consumers and quantity supplied (Q_S) by U.S. producers. Will U.S. consumers of peanuts gain or lose from free trade? _____ Will U.S. producers of peanuts gain or lose from free trade? _____ (Note: Students have the most trouble identifying point Q_S. After checking the answers, do you understand why Q_S is as shown?)

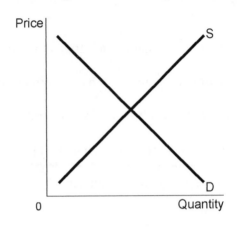

4. Now suppose that U.S. peanut producers successfully convince the government to place a quota on (or to restrict entirely) the import of peanuts into the United States. What is the effect of this on each of the following groups (answer gain, lose, or no change)?

   a. U.S. companies that produce peanuts _____.

   b. U.S. workers in the peanut industry _____.

   c. U.S. consumers of peanuts _____.

   d. U.S. producers of other products for export _____.

   e. the United States as a whole _____.

5. Consider the market for sugar (a primary commodity) produced in Cuba. The relatively steep demand curve suggests that demand is _____. This, combined with the fact that the supply of sugar fluctuates due to weather, implies that sugar prices will _____.

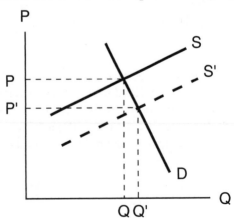

6. (Appendix) Assuming only two countries in the world, the U.S. and Japan, consider the following graph of the market for the U.S. dollar. Assume the equilibrium exchange rate for the U.S. dollar is 130 yen per dollar as indicated.

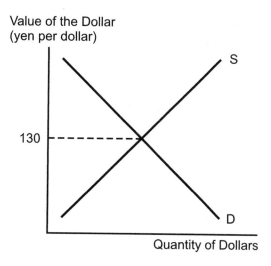

Value of the Dollar
(yen per dollar)

130

Quantity of Dollars

a. Which of the following would result in an increased demand for the dollar? (yes or no)

(i) increased advertising of U.S. products in Japan _____

(ii) more Japanese tourists coming to visit the United States _____

(iii) a rise in U.S. interest rates _____

(iv) more Japanese firms locating in the United States _____

b. Now draw the shift that will occur if there is an increased demand for dollars. What is the effect of this on the value of the dollar relative to the yen? _____ Another way to say this is that the dollar has _____ relative to the yen, or that the yen has _____ relative to the dollar.

SELF-TEST

Multiple-Choice Questions

1. Benefits of trade include:
    a. the efficiency gains from specialization according to comparative advantage.
    b. increased diversity of products.
    c. reduced market power.
    d. all of the above.

2. U.S. trade restrictions on imports may result in:
    a. retaliation.
    b. declining incomes of foreign workers.
    c. higher prices for U.S. consumers.
    d. all of the above.

3. Primary commodities:
    a. are unprocessed raw materials and agricultural products.
    b. generally have inelastic demand.
    c. generally have fluctuating supply.
    d. all of the above.

4. NAFTA stands for:
    a. North American Full Treaty Administration.
    b. New Arms and Free Trade Agreement.
    c. New Association for Floating Exchange Rates and Trade Agreement
    d. North American Free Trade Agreement.

5. One benefit of trade is the improved _____ achieved by specialization according to comparative advantage.
    a. equity.
    b. efficiency.
    c. political stability.
    d. government tax revenue.

6. A country with both total labor cost and labor productivity three times that of another country will have:
    a. much higher labor costs for each unit of production (for example, one radio).
    b. much lower labor costs for each unit of production.
    c. identical costs for each unit of production.
    d. none of the above.

7. The World Trade Organization (WTO):
    a. replaced the General Agreement on Tariffs and Trade (GATT).
    b. manages an international trade agreement.
    c. seeks to reduce tariffs among member countries.
    d. all of the above.

8. A tariff is a:
    a. restriction on the quantity of an imported good.
    b. restriction on the quality of an imported good.
    c. tax on an imported good.
    d. regulation on an imported good.

9. The Group of Eight is:
    a. a group of eight poor countries that suffer greatly from overvalued exchange rates.
    b. a group of eight countries that cooperate in order to stabilize exchange rates.
    c. a group of eight exchange rates that are used to calculate an average.
    d. a group of eight exchange rates that were recently devalued by the less-developed countries.

10. A decline in the prices of exports relative to the prices of imports is the definition of:
    a. a tariff.
    b. an embargo.
    c. declining terms of trade.
    d. declining terms of exchange rates.

11. U.S. exports relative to GDP from 1960 to 2001 have:
    a. increased.
    b. remained amazingly constant.
    c. decreased slightly.
    d. decreased dramatically.

12. (Appendix) Which of the following is *not* true? Rising U.S. interest rates result in:
    a. an increased demand for dollars (internationally).
    b. an appreciation of the dollar relative to foreign currencies.
    c. an appreciation of foreign currencies relative to the dollar.
    d. a greater desire of foreigners to invest in U.S. financial markets.

True-and-False Questions

1. Comparative advantage is defined as a situation whereby a country can produce a good with lower resource cost than another country.

2. Sophisticated capital and technology enhance labor productivity.

3. The calculation of labor costs for a firm must incorporate labor productivity.

4. A quota is a tax on an imported good.

5. If one country has an absolute advantage in the production of both goods compared to another country, then there are no benefits from specialization and exchange for the first country.

6. Declining terms of trade in less developed countries has been eliminated in part by rising market power in the United States.

7. The three members of the North American Free Trade Agreement are the United States, Canada, and Mexico.

8. Absolute advantage may be due to weather, land, and climate.

9. (Appendix) An exchange rate is the price of one country's currency in terms of another country's currency.

10. (Appendix) In a two-country world consisting of the U.S. and France, the supply of dollars by U.S. residents is the same as the demand for francs by U.S. residents.

11. (Appendix) An increase in the value of the dollar makes U.S. exports more expensive to foreigners, who will likely purchase fewer of them.

ANSWERS TO PRACTICE EXERCISES

1. a. U.S., b. U.S., c. U.S., d. Chile, e. yes due to specialization according to comparative advantage—see answer number 2.

2. a. See the graph, b. the United States is better off with trade.

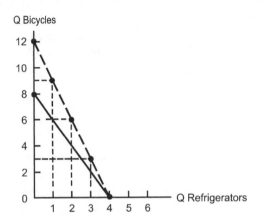

3. See the graph, consumers gain, United States producers lose.

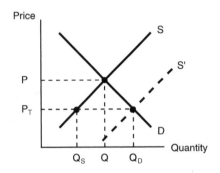

4. a. gain, b. gain, c. lose, d. lose, e. lose

5. inelastic, fluctuate

6. a. (i) yes, (ii) yes, (iii) yes, (iv) yes, b. demand shifts forward, increase, appreciated, depreciated.

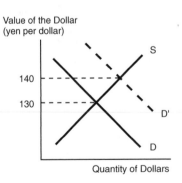

ANSWERS TO SELF-TEST

Multiple-Choice: 1d, 2d, 3d, 4d, 5b, 6c, 7d, 8c, 9b, 10c, 11a, 12c
True-and-False: 1F, 2T, 3T, 4F, 5F, 6F, 7T, 8T, 9T, 10T, 11T

10

Housing

PURPOSE

This chapter discusses U.S. housing policy. It is the first of four chapters that focus on topics that are often considered too important to be left up to the market place alone. The other three chapters focus on health care, agriculture, and social security. Certainly, the topic of housing is important to you, whether you are a current renter or a potential home buyer. Even if you live in a dormitory, you are considered a renter. The major topics are the affordability of housing and U.S. government policy toward housing, housing segregation, and homelessness. One important insight to get from this chapter is a feeling for the effectiveness or ineffectiveness of various types of policies.

LEARNING OBJECTIVES

The learning objectives for this chapter are:

1. to enable you to analyze housing price differentials using supply and demand.

2. to help you to analyze the factors affecting the affordability of home ownership.

3. to inform you about U.S. government policy promoting home ownership.

4. to show you how rental ceilings distort housing markets.

5. to enable you to analyze government programs to house low-income families, such as public housing, subsidies to developers, and rent certificates or vouchers.

6. to illustrate the problem of housing segregation.

7. to discuss the problem of homelessness with you.

8. to help you distinguish between the conservative and liberal viewpoints on housing policy.

STUDY SUGGESTIONS

- As you have done in previous chapters, redraw the graphs in the chapter. Make sure you understand why a curve shifts in a particular way.

- Be sure you realize that for a rental ceiling to be effective, it must be *below* the market equilibrium price. (A price ceiling assists consumers by keeping prices artificially low.) Be sure that you can find the quantity demanded, the quantity supplied, and the shortage that is caused by a rental ceiling on a graph. Remember that you do not shift curves when showing the effects of a price ceiling.

- Be sure you can define each vocabulary term and use it in a sentence.

- Since U.S. government housing policy involves various forms of subsidies, be sure you understand the mortgage interest deduction, subsidies to developers, and subsidies to renters. Who are the gainers from each type of subsidy? Which type of subsidy is most effective in housing low-income families? Which type of subsidy is likely to result in less private low-income housing being available?

Work the following exercises and do the self-test at the end of this section. If you miss a question on the self-test, be sure you understand why you missed it.

PRACTICE EXERCISES

1. On the graph of the River City housing market below, show the effect of an increase in the number of young families in the city. What would be the effect on the average price of a housing unit? _____ What would be the effect on the number of housing units owned? _____

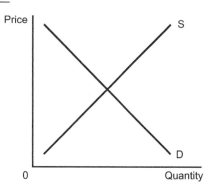

2. Assume that the following are the demand and supply schedules for apartments in Collegetown.

Rent	Quantity Supplied	Quantity Demanded
$800	900	500
700	800	600
600	700	700
500	600	800
400	500	900

a. What is the equilibrium rent? _____ What would be the effect of imposing a rental ceiling of $500? _____

b. Graph the demand and supply schedules and show the effect of the rental ceiling on your graph.

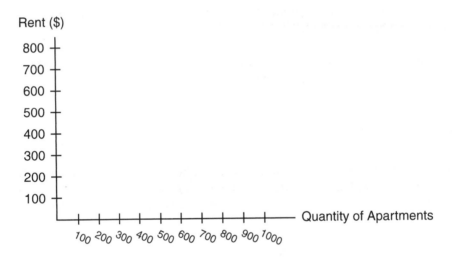

c. Using the example above, explain how rental ceilings interfere with the rationing function of price.

3. City C is composed of 3 equal-sized districts. The following are the percentages of white and black residents in the 3 districts. What is the index of dissimilarity? _____

District	White	African American	Difference
A	80%	20%	60
B	10%	70%	60
C	10%	10%	0

If there were no segregation, what would the index of dissimilarity be? _____ If there were total segregation, what would it be? _____

4. Assume that the fair market rent on an apartment is $600, and its actual rent is the same. A low-income family's income is $800 a month. What would be the amount of subsidy provided the family in a rent voucher? _____

SELF-TEST

Multiple-Choice Questions

1. Which of the following is likely if a city is experiencing an increase in population?
   a. The demand for housing units will decrease.
   b. The price of housing units will decrease.
   c. The supply of housing units will decrease.
   d. The demand for housing units will increase.

2. Since 1970:
   a. the median sales price of a new housing unit has increased.
   b. median household income has increased.
   c. median sales price of new housing relative to median income has increased.
   d. all of the above.

3. The federal income tax deduction of mortgage interest represents a subsidy that mainly goes to:
   a. low-income families.
   b. middle- and high-income families.
   c. all U.S. families equally, regardless of income level.
   d. renters.

4. Among the distortions in the market caused by rental ceilings are:
   a. shortages of low-cost housing units.
   b. increased discrimination against some renters.
   c. deteriorating housing units.
   d. all of the above.

5. When economists say that public housing displaces private housing, they mean that:
   a. the supply of public housing decreases the market price for private housing so that some private housing will be converted to other purposes.
   b. the demand for public housing is so great that it depresses the demand for private housing.
   c. public housing developments use highly desirable land that would be better used for private housing.
   d. public housing concentrates poverty level families in certain areas of the city.

6. Refer to the following graph. A rental ceiling of $350 would cause a:

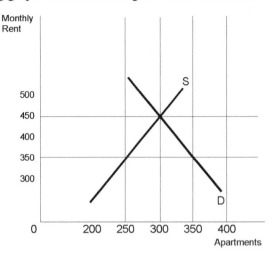

a. shortage of 100 units.
b. surplus of 50 units.
c. surplus of 100 units.
d. shortage of 50 units.

7. Subsidies to developers and public housing programs both benefit:
   a. middle-income families.
   b. the construction industry in addition to poor families who are able to gain housing through these programs.
   c. all renters.
   d. home owners, because they lower the price on new homes.

8. Rental ceilings interfere with the rationing function of price because they:
   a. keep the rent from rising to the equilibrium level.
   b. cause more affordable housing to be supplied.
   c. decrease discrimination against minorities.
   d. decrease the need for rationing by the government.

9. Assume that African Americans and whites are distributed as follows in cities A, B, and C. What would be the index of dissimilarity?

City	African American	White
A	50%	30%
B	30%	20%
C	20%	50%
	100%	100%

   a. 0   b. 30
   c. 60   d. 90

10. Factors causing homelessness include:
    a. personal problems.
    b. unemployment.
    c. the displacement of low-cost housing.
    d. all of the above.

True-and-False Questions

1. When population increases, both the demand for housing and the price of housing increase.

2. A larger percentage of African Americans than whites live in the inner city.

3. Public housing is an inexpensive method of housing poor families.

4. Government and housing advocates agree that there are enough funds allocated to housing programs to help all families who need housing assistance.

5. The interest paid on a mortgage is only slightly more for a 30-year mortgage than it is for a 10-year mortgage.

6. The largest housing subsidy is in the form of rent vouchers for low-income families.

7. An example of a supply-side housing subsidy would be a subsidy to developers.

8. The mortgage interest deduction is a housing subsidy to low-income families.

9. An argument against public housing is that public housing displaces the quantity supplied of private-sector low-cost housing.

10. An argument for demand-side housing subsidies is that the benefits of these subsidies are more certain to go to low-income families than are the benefits of other housing policies.

ANSWERS TO PRACTICE EXERCISES

1. increase demand, average price, and number of units owned

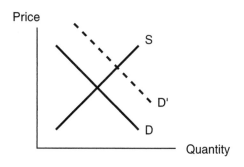

2. a. $600, shortage of 150 apartments; b. see graph below; c. rental ceilings prevent rental rates from rising to the equilibrium level to ration away the shortages

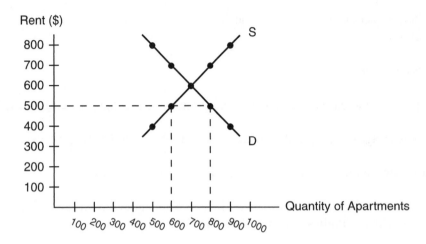

3. $(60 + 60) / 2 = 60, 0, 100.$

4. $.30 \times \$800 = \$240.$ This is the family's share of the rent. $\$600 - \$240 = \$360.$

ANSWERS TO SELF TEST

Multiple-Choice: 1d, 2d, 3b, 4d, 5a, 6a, 7b, 8a, 9b, 10d
True-and-False: 1T, 2T, 3F, 4F, 5F, 6F, 7T, 8F, 9T, 10T

11

Health Care

PURPOSE

This chapter is the second of our four chapters that focus specifically on markets that are too important to leave totally to the marketplace. Indeed, this chapter looks at one of the most important issues in the United States today, health care. Within the last few years, health care has been the topic of a number of bills before Congress. The most commonly discussed issues in U.S. health care are the rising costs of health care, increased resources allocated to health care, inefficiency, and financial access to high-quality health care. The tools we will use to analyze these issues are, once again, the production possibilities curve and supply and demand. Privatization, managed care, and a national health program are among the options discussed.

LEARNING OBJECTIVES

The learning objectives for this chapter are:

1. to acquaint you with the issues of rising costs, increasing resource allocation, limited financial access, and inefficiency in U.S. health care.

2. to introduce you to the principal ways we pay for health care.

3. to help you to understand the roles played by third-party payment, physician sovereignty, rapid technological change, inadequate cost containment, and U.S. attitudes toward health care in terms of expanding resources allocated to health care.

4. to require you to use supply and demand and the production possibilities curve to analyze issues of U.S. health care.

5. to introduce you to some of the commonly proposed policies to decrease the costs of the U.S. health care system.

6. to acquaint you with the liberal and conservative viewpoints toward health care policy.

STUDY SUGGESTIONS

- As you did in previous chapters, be sure that you understand each vocabulary word and can use it in a sentence. Be sure you are using these terms accurately.

- Look at each of the characteristics of health care. Be sure you know if a particular characteristic affects demand or supply. Does that characteristic cause price or usage of health care (or both) to increase?

- Once again, redraw the graphs in the chapter and trace through the shifts of the curves. Be sure you understand why a curve shifts in a particular direction.

- Talk to your family and friends about the health insurance they have. Find out what it costs and what is does or does not cover. See if they are satisfied with their medical care. This is an issue that affects you and your friends. The material has more meaning if you can put it in a personal context.

- As a student, you may be covered through your parents' health insurance and you may receive some degree of coverage through your college or university. Are there "strings" attached to these? For example, do you need to be a full-time student?

- You may lose your health coverage upon graduation from college, and unless you are hired by a firm that provides health coverage for its employees, you may become one of the many people in your age group without health insurance. You will quickly discover that the private purchase of health insurance is incredibly expensive. Have you begun to think about this issue yet? Again, the material is more relevant if you can think about how you will one day be affected.

- There are many statistics cited in this chapter. In general, I tell students that they should try to be aware of "ballpark" numbers for important data (such as the year 2000 share of the population in the United States without any health insurance coverage), trends (such as how spending on health care as a share of GDP has changed in the United States since 1960), and comparisons (such as what minority group in the United States has the highest infant mortality rate). You should check with your instructor to determine whether he or she has the same expectations of you.

- Be sure you understand that when we speak of people without access to any health insurance coverage, we mean people without private coverage purchased by themselves, without coverage from their employers, and without access to government health care programs.

Work the following exercises and take the self-test at the end of this section. If you miss a question on the self-test, be sure you understand why you missed it.

PRACTICE EXERCISES

1. The demand for and supply of hospital beds are shown in the graphs below. Show the effect of each of the following on the graphs and state how equilibrium price and quantity change. (Remember that you should always first indicate the initial equilibrium price and quantity along their respective axes, then shift the appropriate curve, and then answer the question regarding the effect on price and quantity. In each of these questions, you will shift only *one* curve!)

    a. A larger percentage of the population is covered by hospitalization insurance. Effect on equilibrium price? _____ on equilibrium quantity? _____

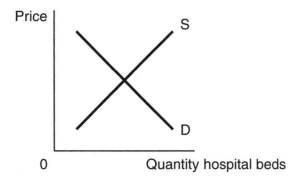

    b. The government establishes a public insurance program covering hospitalization of older citizens. Effect on equilibrium price? _____ on equilibrium quantity? _____

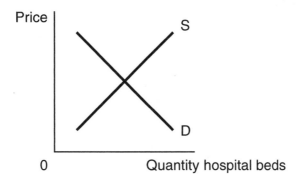

c. Doctors, worried about malpractice suits, check patients who could be treated on an outpatient basis into the hospital. Effect on equilibrium price? _____ on equilibrium quantity? _____

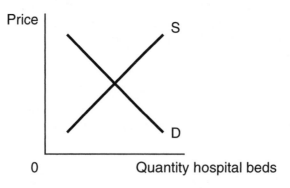

d. Managed care health plans begin to pay for certain medical tests only if these tests are done on an out-patient basis. Patients used to be hospitalized for these tests and the old fee-for-service plans paid for their hospitalization. Effect of the change on equilibrium price? _____ on equilibrium quantity? _____

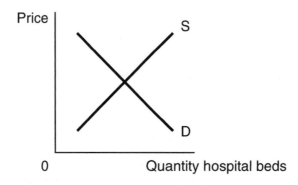

e. A new hospital is built in the community. Effect on equilibrium price? _____ on equilibrium quantity _____?

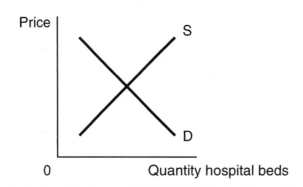

2. A country is at point A below the following production possibilities curve.

    a. Label a point B to which the country might move if it eliminates waste in its health care delivery system.

    b. Move from point B to point C if the country's citizens come to value health care more than most other goods.

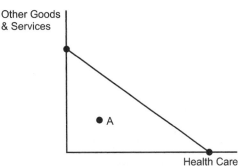

3. With reference to the data presented in the chapter, answer the following.

    a. What were total U.S. health expenditures in 1960? _____ In 2000?_____ U.S health care expenditures in 2000 were about _____ times those of 1960.

    b. As a percent of GDP, U.S. health care expenditures in 1998 were _____. How does this compare with other industrialized countries? _____

    c. How does the U.S. average life expectancy and infant mortality rate compare with those of other industrialized countries?_____

    d. How do infant mortality rates vary among different racial and ethnic groups in the United States?_____ How do they vary in terms of health insurance coverage? _____Do you think there is a relationship between these? _____ What other factors may be involved? _____

SELF-TEST

Multiple-Choice Questions

1. About how much money was spent on health care in the United States in 2000?
    a. $1 billion.
    b. $12 billion.
    c. $160 billion.
    d. $1300 billion.

2. Among the industrialized countries mentioned in the text, which country has the highest health care expenditures as a share of GDP?
    a. France.
    b. United States.
    c. Canada.
    d. the United Kingdom.

3. Approximately what percent of GDP were U.S. health expenditures in 2000?
    a. 5%.
    b. 13%.
    c. 24%.
    d. 55%.

4. Which of the following would be most likely to lack health insurance coverage?
    a. a part-time worker.
    b. a disabled person.
    c. a retired person.
    d. a secretary for a major corporation.

5. Which would be most likely to be covered by Medicare?
    a. a secretary for a major corporation.
    b. a family living below the poverty line.
    c. a person receiving Social Security benefits.
    d. a temporary worker for a small firm.

6. A problem with third-party payment of medical expenses is that:
    a. it leads to overallocation of resources to medical care.
    b. it always restricts the patient's choices.
    c. it inhibits access to medical care.
    d. all of the above.

7. Which of the following contributes to higher health care costs?
    a. patients' attitudes.
    b. third-party payment.
    c. rapid technological change in health care.
    d. all of the above.

8. When we speak of defensive medicine, we mean that:
    a. doctors prescribe treatments which will keep their patients from becoming sick.
    b. doctors prescribe treatments solely because they fear malpractice suits.
    c. doctors donate their services to treat poor patients.
    d. resources are underallocated to health care.

9. Health maintenance organizations:
    a. are the same as fee-for-service health insurance.
    b. are illegal in states with Medicaid programs.
    c. are examples of "managed care."
    d. were a major factor in the increased health care cost between 1960 and 1980.

10. Which of the following is true?
    a. Rising medical costs lead to a greater problem of financial access to health care.
    b. Because so many government programs exist, virtually all low income adults receive adequate health care.
    c. The problem with overallocation of resources to health care is that we value health care too much.
    d. Cost shifting is rare in health care.

11. Which of the industrialized countries mentioned in the text has the highest life expectancy?
     a. the United States.
     b. Japan.
     c. Canada.
     d. the United Kingdom.

12. Which of the following groups in the United States has a higher than average infant mortality rate?
     a. Caucasian.
     b. Native American.
     c. Hispanic.
     d. Asian American.

13. Which of the following increases the demand for health care in the United States?
     a. physician sovereignty.
     b. third party payment.
     c. defensive medicine.
     d. all of the above.

14. Which of the following is an example of the partial privatization of U.S. health care?
     a. medical savings account.
     b. expansion of Medicare and Medicaid.
     c. defensive medicine.
     d. all of the above.

True-and-False Questions

1. Overallocation of resources to health care means that there are other goods and services for which our resources could be used which society would value more.

2. U.S. health care costs have decreased as a percent of our national output.

3. Most Americans who have health insurance coverage acquire it through employment.

4. People living below the poverty line are more likely to lack health insurance coverage than the average American

5. Insurance coverage often determines whether a family has financial access to health care.

6. In recent years, there has been a movement toward various managed care programs in place of traditional fee-for-service insurance in the United States.

7. Defensive medicine decreases the overallocation of resources to health care.

8. Costs of treating indigent patients are often shifted to well-insured patients in the United States.

9. Physician's sovereignty means that the doctor can influence her patients' demand for health care.

10. Canada has the highest per capita health care expenditures in the world, because it has socialized health care.

11. Because the expenditures on health care are the highest in the world, the United States has the highest life expectancies in the world.

12. Because its expenditures on health care are the highest in the world, the United States has the lowest infant mortality rate in the world.

13. Duplication of expensive technology contributes to the high cost of health care in the United States.

14. In 2000, about 4% of the U.S. population was without any form of health insurance coverage.

15. Medicaid is a health care program specifically for low income people.

16. Medicare is a health care program specifically for low income people.

17. Advertising contributes to competition and the privatization of health care.

18. The State Child Health Insurance Program is strictly a federal program of coverage for low income children.

19. Liberals generally support the privatization of U.S. health care.

ANSWERS TO PRACTICE EXERCISES

1. a. increase demand, price, and quantity

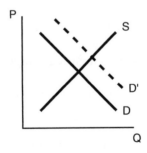

b. increase demand, price, and quantity

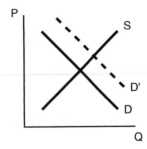

c. increase demand, price, and quantity

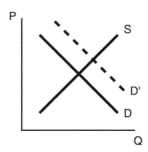

d. decrease demand, price, and quantity

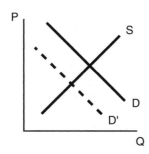

e. increase supply, decrease price, increase quantity

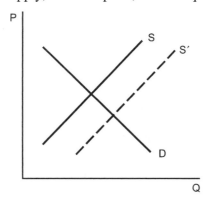

2. a. onto the curve, b. to any point on the curve with more health care

3. READ! Note that the U.S. health care expenditures in 2000 are about 48 times those in 1960.

ANSWERS TO SELF-TEST

Multiple-Choice: 1d, 2b, 3b, 4a, 5c, 6a, 7d, 8b, 9c, 10a, 11b, 12b, 13d, 14a
True-and-False: 1T, 2F, 3T, 4T, 5T, 6T, 7F, 8T, 9T, 10F, 11F, 12F,13T, 14F, 15T, 16F, 17T, 18F, 19F

12

Agriculture

PURPOSE

Chapter 12 discusses the American farm sector, which has a number of unique characteristics, and therefore also has some unique problems. It covers the third of the four "special markets" discussed in the textbook In addition to learning about "the farm problem," you will also consider government price supports (which are an example of a price floor, which is the opposite of the price ceilings discussed in previous chapters). In this chapter, you will also revisit the concept of inelastic demand, which has been an important economic concept throughout the text. The first appendix to the chapter contains a broader discussion of the concept of elasticity, so if your instructor assigns the appendix (or if you want further information), give it careful attention as well. Target prices and deficiency payments are another type of government farm policy and are discussed in the second appendix.

LEARNING OBJECTIVES

The learning objectives for this chapter are:

1. to show you the characteristics of American agriculture.

2. to acquaint you with the history of U.S. agricultural policy.

3. to demonstrate the effects of price supports and other policy choices on production and other variables.

4. to revisit the concept of inelastic demand.

5. to require you to use the supply and demand model to analyze the farm problem and farm policy.

6. to consider the issues of concentration and environmental problems in agriculture.

7. to show you that government policy has both winners and losers, and that the benefits of our farm programs accrue primarily to large corporate producers of agricultural products.

8. to discuss the role of U.S. farm subsidies, food aid, and genetically modified organisms on other countries in the world.

STUDY SUGGESTIONS

- Be sure you understand each vocabulary word and can use each one in a sentence.

- Use common sense—what does demand inelasticity mean? Does it make sense that quantity demanded will not change much when price changes if buyers are not sensitive to price?

- Carefully redraw the graphs in this chapter. They are of great importance in understanding agricultural policy. Remember that with demand and supply graphs, you should first label the equilibrium price and quantity along the appropriate axes, then shift the appropriate curve, and then answer the questions about price and quantity.

- Be sure to understand that price floors (price supports) are designed to help the supplier, in this case the farmer. The goal is to keep the prices they receive for their products artificially high. Keep in mind that you do not shift any curves in the graph of the price floor and continually remind yourself that price floors are "high" and price ceilings are "low" in the graphs (the opposite of what you might want to think).

Work the following exercises and do the self-test at the end of this section. If you miss a question on the self-test, be sure you understand why you missed it.

PRACTICE EXERCISES

1. Graph the following demand and supply schedules for peaches. Indicate the equilibrium price and quantity. Compute the total income of peach growers.

Price (per pound)	Quantity Supplied	Quantity Demanded
$12	1,000,000	500,000
10	850,000	600,000
8	700,000	700,000
6	550,000	800,000
4	400,000	900,000

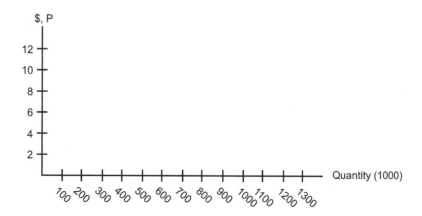

Now assume that growing conditions are ideal and farmers have a bumper crop, so the new supply schedule is below. Add this new supply curve to your graph and show the new equilibrium price and quantity. Calculate the new total income of growers.

Price	Quantity Supplied
$12	1,250,000
10	1,100,000
8	950,000
6	800,000
4	650,000

2. Explain inelastic demand in terms of change in price compared to change in quantity demanded. How does agriculture's inelastic demand contribute to the farm problem?

3. List the gainers and the losers from the following farm policies:

	Gainers	Losers
price supports:		
supply restriction programs:		
target prices with deficiency payments (appendix):		

4. Why have supply restriction programs generally not worked?

5. The supply and demand curves for wheat are shown below. Draw the shift caused by technological advance in growing and harvesting wheat. What will be the effect on the equilibrium price _____ and quantity of wheat? _____

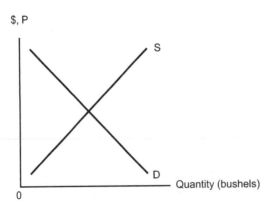

6. Consider the market for corn, with demand and supply shown below. If the government price support is $3 per bushel of corn, label the new quantity demanded Q_D and the new quantity supplied Q_S along the quantity axis. What is the problem that will result from the price support? _____

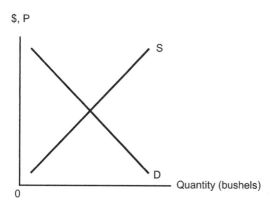

7. The supply and inelastic demand for sorghum are shown below. Assume that exceptionally good weather results in a bumper crop of sorghum. Shift the proper curve to show this. What is the change in price? _____ in quantity? _____ Which change is larger? _____

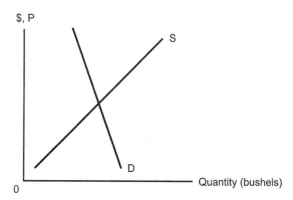

8. Write a paragraph comparing and contrasting the liberal and conservative viewpoints on U.S. farm policy.

SELF-TEST

Multiple-Choice Questions

1. When we say that demand is inelastic, we mean that:
    a. buyers are very responsive to changes in price.
    b. if price changes, the percentage change in quantity demanded will be smaller than the percentage change in price.
    c. if price changes, the percentage change in quantity demanded will be greater than the percentage change in price.
    d. farmers cannot stretch their fixed costs over more output.

The following two questions refer to the following graph for a hypothetical market for grain sorghum.

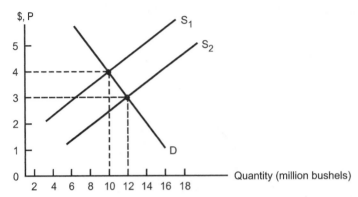

2. Initially assume that supply is S_1. What is market equilibrium price and total income of the farmers?
    a. $4, $48 million.   b. $4, $40 million.
    c. $3, $40 million.   d. $4, $36 million.

3. Now assume that supply increases to S_2. What is market equilibrium price and total income of the farmers?
    a. $4, $40 million.   b. $3, $30 million.
    c. $3, $36 million.   d. $4, $48 million.

4. Since the demand for most farm products is inelastic:
    a. the demand curve will be relatively steep.
    b. buyers are relatively unresponsive to changes in price.
    c. total farm income will decrease if the market price falls.
    d. all of the above.

5. What did the PIK program, the Soil Bank, and the CRP program have in common?
    a. They all are price support programs.
    b. They are all supply restriction programs.
    c. They all seek to increase the demand for farm products.
    d. They all limit imports of farm products.

Answer the following two questions on the basis of the following hypothetical data for soybeans.

Price (per bushel)	Quantity Supplied	Quantity Demanded
$14	15,000,000	10,000,000
12	13,500,000	11,000,000
10	12,000,000	12,000,000
8	10,500,000	13,000,000
6	9,000,000	14,000,000

6. Market equilibrium price and quantity are:
    a. $12, 11,000,000.   b. $10, 12,000,000.
    c. $12, 13,500,000.   d. $8, 13,000,000.

7. If the government price support for soybeans is $14 per bushel, there will be a:
    a. shortage of 5,000,000.
    b. surplus of 3,000,000.
    c. surplus of 5,000,000.
    d. surplus of 2,000,000.

8. The major liberal criticism of government payments to farmers is that:
    a. the greatest share of government payments has gone to large farms.
    b. payments have caused great inefficiency.
    c. payments have slowed the exodus of people from agriculture.
    d. farm programs have interfered with the workings of the market.

9. (Appendix question) Unlike price supports, target prices:
    a. do not create surpluses.
    b. lower the price of U.S. farm exports.
    c. lower the price of food to consumers.
    d. all of the above.

10. The three unique economic characteristics of agriculture are:
    a. elastic demand, extensive technological change, and immobile resources.
    b. inelastic demand, extensive technological change, and immobile resources.
    c. inelastic demand, extensive technological change, and very mobile resources.
    d. elastic demand, extensive technological change, and very mobile resources.

11. Price fluctuation in short-run agricultural markets results from:
    a. inelastic demand.
    b. changing weather.
    c. fluctuating supply.
    d. all of the above.

12. Price supports
    a. encourage over-production.
    b. encourage under-consumption.
    c. create surpluses.
    d. all of the above.

True-and-False Questions

1. Less than two percent of the U.S. population is engaged in farming.

2. Government farm programs have contributed to the increasing concentration in agriculture.

3. The "Freedom to Farm" Act of 1996 eliminated price supports and target prices on all agricultural commodities.

4. Extensive technological change in agriculture has caused the real price of farm products to fall over time.

5. Relatively small increases in supply can cause large decreases in price because the demand for agricultural products is inelastic.

6. Supply restriction programs have been extremely effective in decreasing the supply of farm products.

7. There are many other uses for most farmland if it is not farmed.

8. Farm incomes rise when farm prices fall because farmers sell more of their products at the lower prices.

9. The government establishes price supports when it sets Commodity Credit Corporation loan rates.

10. The basic agricultural problem is that we simply overallocate resources to agriculture.

11. The inelastic demand for farm products results in price instability in the short run.

12. The long-run problem in agriculture is declining market farm prices.

13. Technological advance contributed to the long-run price declines in agriculture.

14. Price supports create shortages.

15. *Little House on the Prairie* is an accurate image of most U.S. agriculture.

16. The food stamp program is an example of a program used to increase the demand for farm products.

17. According to the text, genetically modified organisms will be the solution to world hunger.

18. (Appendix question). With inelastic demand, the percentage change in quantity demanded is less than the percentage change in price.

ANSWERS TO PRACTICE EXERCISES

1. $8, 700,000, $8 × 700,000 = $5,600,000; $6, 800,000, $6 × 800,000 = $4,800,000.

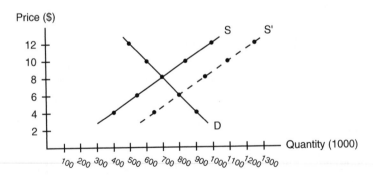

2. Inelasticity means that the percentage change in quantity demanded is smaller than the percentage change in price. Small changes in supply can cause big changes in price, and farm prices tend to be unstable as a result.

3. price supports: gainers = farmers, losers = taxpayers and consumers
    supply restriction: gainers = farmers, losers = taxpayers and consumers
    target prices: gainers = farmers and consumers, losers = taxpayers

4. farmers put least productive land into such programs and farm the rest more intensively

5. increase supply, decrease price, increase quantity

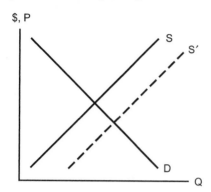

6. a surplus

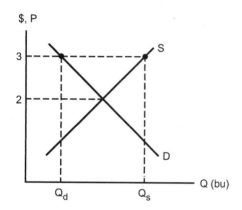

7. increase supply, decrease price, increase quantity, change in price is larger

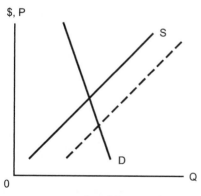

8. Conservatives believe the government should never have gotten involved in farming and that the programs were misguided, inefficient, and expensive. Liberals agree with much of those criticisms, but defend the programs on the basis that they made the transfer of people out of agriculture since the 1930s more orderly.

ANSWERS TO SELF-TEST

Multiple-Choice: 1b, 2b, 3c, 4d, 5b, 6b, 7c, 8a, 9d, 10b, 11d, 12d
True-and-False: 1T, 2T, 3F, 4T, 5T, 6F, 7F, 8F, 9T, 10T, 11T, 12T, 13T, 14F, 15F, 16T, 17F, 18T

13

Social Security

PURPOSE

Our purpose in Chapter 12 is to discuss the U.S. Social Security system. In this chapter we move onto our fourth "special market," which entails the care for our nation's elderly and disabled. I know that many of you are concerned about whether Social Security will still be there when you are ready to retire. We also know that the public has many misconceptions about the Social Security system. We therefore look at the structure of the Social Security system and many of the issues and problems with Social Security, as well as some of the changes likely to occur in the system over the next few years.

LEARNING OBJECTIVES

The learning objectives in this chapter are:

1. to acquaint you with the history of the Social Security system.

2. to acquaint you with the features of the Social Security system.

3. to help you differentiate between social insurance, private insurance, and public assistance programs.

4. to discuss with you the long-run problem of Social Security.

5. to help you understand some of the measures taken, or likely to be taken, to increase the financial viability of Social Security.

6. to discuss with you the women's issues inherent in Social Security.

7. to discuss with you many of the other issues surrounding Social Security.

8. to delineate the conservative and liberal viewpoints on Social Security, including the current proposals of President George Bush.

STUDY SUGGESTIONS

- As with all other chapters, be sure that you understand the vocabulary words and can use them in a sentence.

- Social Security is a system that affects us all. Talk to your family, friends, and coworkers about Social Security. See if their attitudes mirror those in the chapter. While reading the chapter, try to discover whether any of them are incorrect.

- As you read through the chapter, make sure you understand the differences between social insurance, private insurance, and public assistance programs. Tables 13-1 and 13-2 will be very helpful to you.

Work the following practice exercises and take the self-test. If you miss a question on the test, be sure you understand why.

PRACTICE EXERCISES

1. Jane's salary the last year she was employed was $25,000. Her Social Security retirement benefits totaled $10,800 the first year she was retired. John's salary the last year of employment was $78,000. In his first year of retirement, he received $18,000 in Social Security retirement benefits.

    a. Find the replacement rates for both Jane _____ and John _____.

    b. Would you characterize their retirement benefits as progressive, regressive, or proportional? _____ Why? _____

2. Jane paid Social Security payroll tax on her salary of $25,000. In addition to her salary, she received income of $185 interest on a passbook savings account. John paid Social Security payroll tax on the maximum earnings taxable for Social Security, which were $60,000 that year. In addition to his $78,000 salary John received income of $9,000 from investments. The Social Security tax rate was 6.2 percent.

    a. Calculate both Jane's _____ and John's _____ Social Security tax.

    b. What percent of the total income did the tax amount for Jane? _____ for John? _____

    c. Was the tax progressive, proportional, or regressive? _____ Why? _____

3. Answer the following questions about Social Security.

    a. In addition to old age (retirement), what does Social Security insure against?

    b. How long must a worker pay Social Security taxes before being eligible for retirement benefits?

    c. If a worker could receive retirement benefits of $800 a month on her own work record or one-half her husband's $1800 a month, which benefit would she automatically be paid?

4. List the arguments for and against making Social Security voluntary.

5. Analyze the "bad buy" argument, presenting both sides of the issue.

6. Explain the long-run problem with Social Security. Then list at least five of the measures that can be taken to solve the problem.

SELF-TEST

Multiple-Choice Questions

1. Social Security is a government:
    a. public assistance program aimed at alleviating poverty among aged Americans.
    b. social insurance program that insures covered workers against death, disability, and old age.
    c. social insurance program that covers only retired workers.
    d. transfer program that provides income and subsidized medical care to Americans over the age of fifty-five.

2. The last year he is employed, Jim earns $50,000. In his first year of retirement, his Social Security benefits are $15,000. His replacement rate is:
   a. 20%.   b. 30%.   c. 50%.   d. 100%.

3. Which of the following is correct?
   a. Both Social Security benefits and taxes are regressive.
   b. Both Social Security benefits and taxes are proportional.
   c. Social Security benefits are progressive, but Social Security taxes are regressive.
   d. Social Security benefits are progressive, but Social Security taxes are proportional.

4. When we speak of Social Security's "widow's income gap," we are talking about the situation by which the dependent spouse of a deceased worker:
   a. no longer receives benefits after her youngest child reaches the age of sixteen, but cannot receive retirement benefits until she reaches the age of sixty.
   b. has difficulty drawing survivorship benefits because applying for Social Security benefits is a slow, cumbersome process.
   c. stops receiving survivorship benefits if she goes to work.
   d. stops receiving survivorship benefits if she remarries.

5. When we say that the Social Security retirement trust fund will be exhausted by 2037, we mean that:
   a. Social Security will go bankrupt in 2037 if we don't do something soon.
   b. after 2037 Social Security will go back to being a strictly pay-as-you go system.
   c. Social Security will not pay any benefits after 2037.
   d. people who are already retired in 2037 will continue to receive benefits, but people who retire after 2037 will not receive benefits.

6. An argument against making Social Security voluntary is that:
   a. adverse selection would increase the costs of the program.
   b. some people would neither save for their retirement nor participate in Social Security.
   c. public assistance costs would increase.
   d. all of the above.

7. The argument that workers save less because Social Security lessens their need to save privately for their retirement is the:
   a. early retirement effect.
   b. retirement effect.
   c. Social Security wealth effect.
   d. reduced savings effect.

8. Some of the steps that can be taken to increase the financial soundness of Social Security are to:
   a. fully tax benefits, lower the normal and early retirement ages, and increase the Social Security tax rate.
   b. stop taxing benefits , raise the normal and early retirement ages, and decrease the Social Security tax rate.
   c. fully tax benefits, raise the normal and early retirement ages, and decrease the Social Security tax rate.
   d. fully tax benefits, raise the normal and early retirement ages, and increase the Social Security tax rate.

9. In a pay-as-you-go insurance plan:
    a. benefits are mainly financed from current tax revenues.
    b. benefits are mainly financed from investment income on taxes collected previously.
    c. the plan must have assets to cover all expected benefits that it will have to pay in the future.
    d. benefits depend on premiums paid in the past.

10. The principle of "individual equity" implies that:
    a. benefits should be paid strictly on the basis of need.
    b. benefits should be proportional to taxes paid.
    c. benefits should be paid to put a minimum floor of income under all citizens.
    d. benefits should not depend on taxes paid in the past.

11. When we say that the Social Security tax is regressive, we mean that:
    a. the tax takes a larger percent of the income of high-income people than low-income people.
    b. the tax takes the same percent of income from high-income and low-income people.
    c. the tax takes a larger percent in income from low-income people than from high-income people.
    d. none of the above.

12. Which of the following is an example of a public assistance program?
    a. Social Security.
    b. Medicare.
    c. welfare.
    d. all of the above.

13. A major difference between a public insurance program and a public assistance program is that:
    a. a public assistance program involves the government, whereas a public insurance program does not.
    b. a public assistance program targets the needy, whereas a public insurance program does not.
    c. a public assistance program is financed by payroll taxes, whereas a public insurance program is not.
    d. a public insurance program stigmatizes the poor, whereas a public assistance program does not.

True-and-False Questions

1. The long-run problem with Social Security is that the government is raising the normal retirement age.

2. The replacement rate is higher for low-income workers than high-income workers.

3. The early retirement age is the lowest age that a worker can receive full retirement benefits from Social Security.

4. Social Security retirement benefits are based on the worker's three years of highest earnings.

5. Social insurance programs are usually voluntary.

6. Social insurance programs are supported by the premiums paid by participants.

7. When the Social Security retirement trust fund is exhausted, the system will still be able to pay benefits equal to 72 percent of the current level, if nothing is done to reform the Social Security system.

8. Equal amounts of Social Security taxes are paid by the worker and the employer.

9. The Social Security trust funds are invested in risky securities.

10. Social Security is a welfare program.

11. Privatization means the transfer of assets or responsibility from the private sector of the economy to the government.

12. An entitlement is a payment to which eligible citizens have a right to receive based on U.S. law.

13. Social security recipients live on a "fixed income."

14. Both social insurance and private insurance are voluntary.

15. Social security is financed by a tax on both workers and their employees.

16. A pay-as-you-go system is one that collects taxes from people in the early years as they are working, saves this revenue, and then uses it for the same people in their later years when they retire.

17. "Individual equity" means that you receive benefits because you are poor.

18. The normal retirement age is 65.

19. Capital gains, interest income, stock dividends, and other forms of income that are not earned by working are taxed for Social Security at the same rate as earnings from work.

20. The average age of the population in the United States is increasing.

21. Adverse selection would be a problem with a voluntary social insurance program.

ANSWERS TO PRACTICE EXERCISES

1. a. Jane: 43.2%, John: 23.1%, b. progressive (larger % of low-earner Jane's income was replaced)

2. a. Jane: $1550, John: $3720, b. Jane: 6.15%, John: 4.28%, c. regressive (takes larger % of low-income Jane's income)

3. a. death and disability, b. 40 quarters (10 years), c. $900, one-half spouse's benefits

4. For: economic freedom, worker could do better investing on his/her own, limitation of government role in our lives
    Against: some people would not save and others earn so little they could not save, welfare cost would increase, adverse selection would increase the costs of the program.

5. Bad buy argument: If we credit both the employer's and the worker's shares of Social Security taxes to the worker and then only consider retirement benefits, Social Security is a bad buy for some (young, high income) workers. They could do better investing these taxes privately.
    If we consider only the worker's taxes and also consider disability and death (survivorship) benefits, Social Security is not a bad buy.

6. Declining worker/beneficiary ratio
    Raise normal and early retirement ages, increase taxes, decrease benefits, invest trust funds in stock market, fully tax benefits, partially or fully privatize

ANSWERS TO SELF-TEST

Multiple-Choice: 1b, 2b, 3c, 4a, 5b, 6d, 7c, 8d, 9a, 10b 11c, 12c, 13b
True-and-False: 1F, 2T, 3F, 4F, 5F, 6F, 7T, 8T, 9F, 10F, 11F, 12T, 13F, 14F, 15T, 16F, 17F, 18T, 19F, 20T, 21T

14

Unemployment and Inflation

PURPOSE

We now come to the first of three chapters focused on the stability of our economy. The purpose of this chapter is to help you consider the topics of unemployment and inflation, their causes, their types, and their effects. This is done in the context of an introduction to the macro economy. We will also consider another example of a price floor (similar to the price supports discussed in the agriculture chapter). In the context of a labor market, the price floor is the minimum wage.

LEARNING OBJECTIVES

The learning objectives for this chapter are:

1. to introduce you to the concepts of unemployment and inflation.

2. to clarify the meaning of the labor force participation rate, the unemployment rate, the consumer price index, and the inflation rate, as well as recent data for these variables.

3. to help you compare the labor force participation rates for men and women, different time periods, and different countries.

4. to help you consider the likelihood of unemployment for people in different racial, ethnic, gender, and age groups.

5. to help you to assess the employment effects of immigration and the minimum wage.

6. to help you consider the effects of inflation on different groups of people.

7. to assist you in analyzing the reasons for unemployment and inflation, and the severity of their effects on the economy.

8. to help you establish the macroeconomic context within which you can analyze policy to reduce these problems in the next chapter.

STUDY SUGGESTIONS

- Always think through the definitions of each vocabulary word to be sure you understand its meaning and can use it in a sentence.

- As you read about how to calculate the labor force participation rate and the unemployment rate, you need to drop any preconceived notions you may have about how they are calculated. Be sure you understand the meaning of unemployment (those not working, but actively seeking employment), as well as the meaning of the labor force (the total number of people who are employed plus the total number of people who are unemployed). Be sure you understand that people not seeking employment, including retirees, students, full time homemakers, children, discouraged workers, etc. are not called unemployed people. Part-time workers are defined as employed, just as if they are working full time.

- If your instructor expects you to calculate unemployment rates, labor-force participation rates, or inflation rates, be sure you know how to translate a rate that is expressed as a decimal into one that is expressed as a percentage. For example, if a rate = 0.15, translate it into a percentage by moving the decimal point two places to the right and add a percentage sign. (That is, 0.15 = 15%.)

- Keep in mind that full employment does not mean no unemployment; it means no *cyclical* unemployment.

- Keep in mind that when you use a supply and demand graph to analyze the effect of a minimum wage, you do not shift a curve. Instead, you label the quantity demanded and quantity supplied of labor that correspond to the minimum wage along the employment (number of workers) axis. As with any price floor, the minimum wage is designed to help suppliers (of labor in this case). Remember that to be effective, the minimum wage must be placed high in the graph; that is, above the equilibrium price.

- When you work with the demand and supply graph in the context of immigration, be sure that you first label the original price and quantity, shift the one appropriate curve, and then answer the questions about price and quantity.

- In this as well as other chapters that contain many statistics, unless your instructor tells you otherwise, you should try to remember "ballpark" numbers of important data (such as the current unemployment rate), trends (such as rising labor force participation rate), and comparisons (such as which minority has the highest unemployment rate).

Work through the following exercises and do the self-test at the end of this section. If you miss a question on the self-test, make sure you understand why you missed it.

PRACTICE EXERCISES

1. Consider the population of a small country with the following statistics. Calculate the unemployment rate _____ and labor force participation rate. _____

    total population = 700
    children under age 16 = 100
    elderly retired people = 170
    full time students = 75
    full time homemakers = 45
    people working full time for pay = 150
    people working part time for pay = 120
    people not working but seeking employment = 30
    people not working but have given up seeking employment = 10

2. Looking into the future, consider a country with the following data and calculate the year 2020 inflation rate. _____

    year 2020 CPI = 220
    year 2019 CPI = 200

3. Consider the graph of a low-skill labor market, where D is the demand for low-skilled workers by business firms, and S is the supply of native-born U.S. workers who offer their labor services in the low-skill labor market. Show the shift that occurs with large-scale immigration of low-skilled workers into the United States. What is the effect on the wage rate? _____ on overall employment? _____ on employment of native-born workers? _____

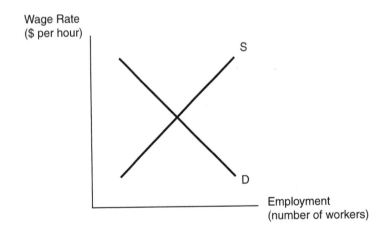

4. Consider the graph of a low-skill labor market, where D is the demand for low-skilled workers and S is the supply of low-skilled workers. The equilibrium wage rate is W_0. Label an effective minimum wage along the wage axis. Label the new quantity demanded of labor Q_D and the new quantity supplied of labor Q_S along the employment axis. What is the economic problem that results? _____

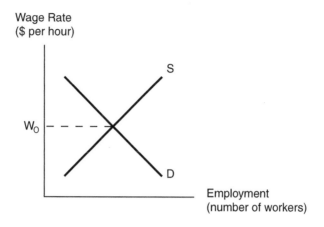

5. By now you surely remember where to place a point labeled "U" to represent unemployment in the production possibilities curve below. Do so now! What is the problem that results for the economy as a whole? _____

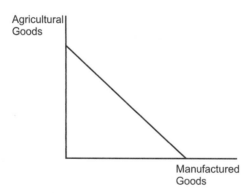

6. (Appendix) What is the value of the consumer price index for the year 2050 if the weighted average price of a fixed basket of consumer goods is $6,000 in year 2050 and $3,000 in the base year? _____

SELF-TEST

Multiple-Choice Questions

1. Which of the following are macroeconomic topics?
    a. inflation.
    b. cyclical unemployment.
    c. the overall economy.
    d. all of the above.

2. Since 1964, the U.S. labor force participation rate has:
   a. increased.
   b. decreased.
   c. remained constant.
   d. we don't know.

3. According to the official definition of unemployment, unemployed people include those who:
   a. have given up seeking employment.
   b. are working only part time.
   c. are not working but are actively seeking employment.
   d. all of the above.

4. The labor force is defined to include:
   a. unemployed people.
   b. full time employed people.
   c. part time employed people.
   d. all of the above.

5. Discouraged workers are those who:
   a. are unsatisfied in their current job.
   b. are easily discouraged and quit their jobs.
   c. have given up seeking employment.
   d. have given up hopes of finding a better job than the one they have now.

6. Which of the following is *not* true? Unemployment rates are above the national average for:
   a. Whites.
   b. Hispanics.
   c. Blacks.
   d. teens (age 16 and over).

7. A young man experiences a short delay in finding his first job after graduating from high school. This type of unemployment is:
   a. frictional.
   b. structural.
   c. cyclical.
   d. none of the above.

8. A middle-aged steelworker is laid off from her job after increased imports of steel reduce the need for U.S. steelworkers, even while increased exports of aircraft increase the need for U.S. aerospace engineers. This type of unemployment is:
   a. frictional.
   b. structural.
   c. cyclical.
   d. none of the above.

9. As the nation enters recession, the number of jobs declines and people are laid off. This type of unemployment is:
   a. frictional.
   b. structural.
   c. cyclical.
   d. none of the above.

10. Which of the following is *not* an appropriate policy to address structural unemployment?
    a. macroeconomic policies to expand the economy and create more jobs.
    b. training and education programs.
    c. relocation assistance.
    d. provision of mass transit and childcare facilities.

11. What are the effects of a minimum wage in a low-skill occupation?
    a. a larger quantity supplied of labor.
    b. a smaller quantity demanded of labor.
    c. a surplus of labor (unemployment).
    d. all of the above.

12. The cost of unemployment to the macro economy is:
    a. foregone output.
    b. individual hardship.
    c. higher prices.
    d. higher interest rates.

13. Inflation generally causes:
    a. a decline in purchasing power for the nation as a whole.
    b. a redistribution of purchasing power within the nation.
    c. a reduced ability of all to afford to buy goods and services.
    d. harm to social security recipients.

14. Which of the following is *not* true? Hyperinflation generally occurs:
    a. due to severe distortions to the economy.
    b. due to factors such as wars.
    c. due to normal events in an economy.
    d. due to factors such as revolutions.

15. The U.S. labor force participation is approximately:
    a. 45%.
    b. 65%.
    c. 85%.
    d. 95%.

16. Which of the following groups has the highest unemployment rate in the United States?
    a. youth (age 16-18).
    b. African Americans.
    c. Hispanics.
    d. Asian Americans.

True-and-False Questions

1. Gross domestic product (GDP) is the total output of an economy.

2. Labor force participation rates currently are higher for women than for men.

3. The current unemployment rate is about 10%.

4. Frictional unemployment is assumed to be a very serious problem.

5. Structural unemployment involves a mismatch between unemployed workers and available jobs.

6. Full employment means there is no cyclical unemployment.

7. Large-scale immigration of low-skilled workers may reduce wages in low-skill occupations.

8. The inflation rate based on the consumer price index (CPI) is generally assumed to overstate inflation.

9. Inflation causes redistribution of well-being within our economy.

10. Profit-push inflation occurs when any sectors of the economy increase their demand for goods and services.

11. Rising energy prices in the 1970s resulted in cost-push inflation in the U.S.

12. The current inflation rate is very low.

13. People often resort to barter during periods of hyperinflation.

14. (Appendix) The consumer price index (CPI) for the base year will always be 100.

15. Surprisingly, unemployment rates for teenagers (ages 16 and over) are very low.

16. The Earned Income Credit could be used to supplement the earnings of low-wage workers in a way that avoids some of the problems associated with minimum wage.

17. The current inflation rate is under 2% per year.

ANSWERS TO PRACTICE EXERCISES

1. The unemployment rate = 10%. Divide the total number of unemployed people (30) by the number of unemployed people + the number of people employed at least part time for pay (150 + 120). Thus, the unemployment rate is: 30 / (30 + 120 + 150) = 30 / 300 = .10 = 10%.

    The labor force participation rate = 50%. Divide the number of people in the labor force (300) by the total number of people in the population aged 16 or over (700-100). Thus the labor force participation rate is: 300 / 600 = .50 = 50%.

    (Remember that to translate a decimal to a percentage, simply move the decimal point over two places and add a percentage sign.)

2. $$\frac{220 - 200}{200} = \frac{20}{200} = 0.10 = 10\%$$

3. increase the supply of labor, decrease the wage rate, increase overall employment, decrease employment of native-born workers

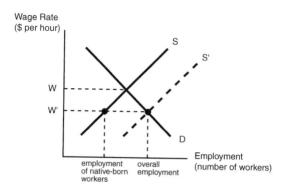

4. surplus of labor (unemployment)

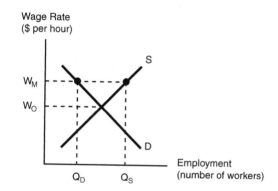

5. The problem is reduced output (GDP).

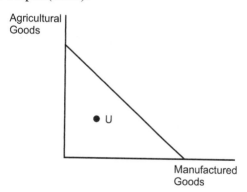

6. 2050 CPI = (6000 / 3000) × 100 = 200

ANSWERS TO SELF-TEST

Multiple-Choice: 1d, 2a, 3c, 4d, 5c, 6a, 7a, 8b, 9c, 10a, 11d, 12a, 13b, 14c, 15b, 16a
True-and-False: 1T, 2F, 3F, 4F, 5T, 6T, 7T, 8T, 9T, 10F, 11T, 12T, 13T, 14T, 15F, 16T, 17

15

Government Macroeconomic Policy

PURPOSE

This is the second of the "stability" chapters and its purpose is to introduce you to the concepts of the macro economy, macroeconomic policy, and macroeconomic issues. This is a chapter that will heighten your interest in our economy overall. You've probably heard the terms fiscal policy, monetary policy, and supply-side policy. Most likely, you (and the rest of the American public) have very little understanding of what these policies mean and how they affect our economy. They maybe sound too complex to you. And you may have very little understanding of the liberal vs. conservative philosophies when it comes to these policies. In this chapter, you will use simple graphs (building on the demand and supply analysis we've been using all along) to acquire a sophisticated understanding of our macro economy and the policies affecting it. It will not be as difficult as you might think!

LEARNING OBJECTIVES

The learning objectives for this chapter are:

1. to acquaint you with the graph of aggregate demand and aggregate supply.

2. to help you understand the concept of gross domestic product, its measurement, and its limitations.

3. to acquaint you with the difference between real and nominal GDP.

4. to help you understand what sectors are represented by aggregate demand, as well as the factors that would shift the aggregate demand and aggregate supply curves.

5. to relate the concepts of unemployment and inflation, as well as the types of inflation discussed in Chapter 14, to the aggregate demand and aggregate supply graph.

6. to assist you in understanding the basic workings of fiscal, monetary, and supply-side policy, as well as recent economic policy and proposals, and the liberal and conservative philosophies about policy.

STUDY SUGGESTIONS

- Always read the definition of each vocabulary word, and be sure you can use it in a sentence.

- Always, always, always redraw the graphs in the text. This will help you be sure you understand the material, and you will be more likely to remember it for an exam.

- You are already familiar with the graph of demand and supply. This chapter allows you to make a transition from the analysis of markets (with demand and supply) to an analysis of the macro economy (with aggregate demand and aggregate supply). The macro economy is just our total economy, rather than the individual markets within it. As with demand and supply, generally think of shifts in aggregate demand (AD) and aggregate supply (AS) as forward and backward shifts, not up or down. This is especially important when shifting AS.

- Also remember that a forward shift (or a shift to the right) is an increase, while a backward shift (or a shift to the left) is a decrease. Think in terms of the GDP axis.

- Keep in mind that aggregate means total. This means that AD is to total demand for U.S. GDP and aggregate supply is the total supply of U.S. GDP. Always remember the four sectors represented by aggregate demand are consumers, businesses, government, and foreign purchasers. This will help you when you attempt to think through the effects of fiscal and monetary policy.

- Keep in mind that when we are talking about purchases (that is, spending by consumers, businesses, foreigners, or government), we are talking about aggregate demand. Do not confuse, for example, government purchases of national defense (i.e. spending on national defense) with the production or supply of national defense. In other words, only shift the AD curve when there is a change in *purchases*. As an example, draw the graph of aggregate demand and aggregate supply. Draw the shift that will occur if there is an increase in government purchases of public libraries. This should cause an increase in AD, and therefore an increase in GDP, and employment, and the average price level. Did you do it correctly?

- Keep in mind that there is no necessary relationship between government spending and taxes. For example, if government spending increases, taxes need not increase in order to finance the increased spending (since the government can also borrow money). In all of the problems, assume that taxes do not change unless stated otherwise.

- Keep in mind that monetary policy affects the aggregate demand curve, and not the aggregate supply curve. Students often show the effect of expansionary monetary policy as a forward shift in aggregate supply (I think this is because they link money *supply* and aggregate *supply* in their minds). Expansionary monetary policy shifts the AGGREGATE DEMAND CURVE forward; contractionary monetary policy shifts the AGGREGATE DEMAND CURVE backward. As an example, draw the graph of aggregate demand and aggregate supply. Draw the shift that will occur if the Federal Reserve reduces the nation's money supply. This should cause a decrease (backwards shift) in AD, and therefore a decrease in GDP, employment, and the average price level. Did you do it correctly?

- Remember that in the graph of the macro economy, GDP and employment move together. (That is, an increase in GDP means an increase in employment, and vice versa.)

- Always remember, whenever you are asked to determine the effect of policy on the macro economy (just as when you were asked to determine the effect of some change on a particular market), *first* label the initial average price level and level of GDP along their respective axes (if this has not already been done), then shift the curve, and *then* determine the effect on P, GDP, and employment. Also remember that you will be shifting only one curve!

- Be sure you understand EVEYTHING about the AD and AS curve shifts. If you get just one little part of it wrong, this is still serious as you don't understand the entire picture.

Work through the practice exercises and take the self test. Make sure you understand any questions you may have missed.

PRACTICE EXERCISES

1. Draw the shift that will occur if there is a decrease in government income transfers, which decrease the incomes of many consumers. What will be the effect on GDP and employment? _____ What will be the effect on the average price level? _____

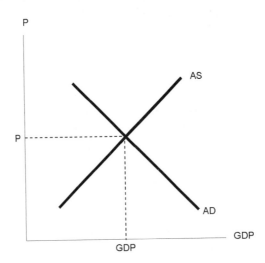

(Be very careful to distinguish between changes in transfers as a fiscal policy tool vs. a supply-side policy tool. Since this question refers to the impact of transfers on *consumer incomes*, we know it will be a fiscal policy tool in this example, because it involves *consumer purchases*.)

2. Draw the shift that will occur if there is an increase in government purchases of police protection services. What will be the effect on GDP and employment? _____ What will be the effect on the average price level? _____

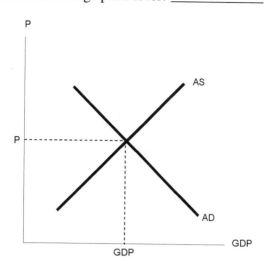

(Be sure to realize we are talking about purchases in question #2 and not greater production or supply of police protection. You should be shifting aggregate demand and not aggregate supply.)

3. Draw the shift that will occur when the government increases regulations requiring pollution controls on automobiles, thereby raising the costs of production. What will be the effect on GDP and employment? _____ What will be the effect on the average price level? _____

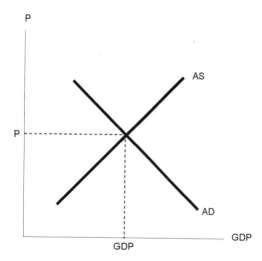

(Keep in mind that an increase in government regulations generally makes it more difficult and expensive to produce. It reduces the *incentive* to produce. This clues you in that the aggregate supply curve will shift, and the aggregate demand curve will not.)

4. Draw the shift that will occur if there is an increase in tax rates, which we will assume results
    in reduced work incentives and work effort by the labor force. What will be the effect on
    GDP and employment? _____ What will be the effect on the average price level?
    _____

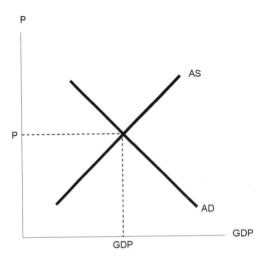

5. Draw the shift that will occur if there is an increase in taxes, which serve to decrease the
    after-tax income of consumers. What will be the effect on GDP and employment?
    _____ What will be the effect on the average price level? _____

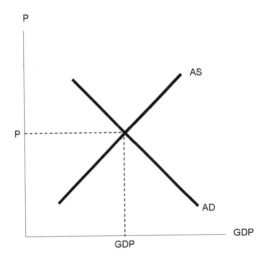

(Note: Do you understand the difference between questions #4 and #5? In question #4, the
increase in tax rates affects aggregate supply, since it operates on work incentives and effort.
In question #5, the increase in taxes is a fiscal policy tool, since it affects consumers' after-
tax income and therefore their purchases.)

6. Draw the shift that will occur if the government reduces transfers, which we will assume results in greater work incentives and work effort by the labor force. What will be the effect on GDP and employment? _____ What will be the effect on the average price level? _____

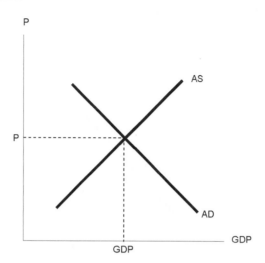

(Note: Do you understand the difference between questions #6 and #1? In question #6, the reduction in transfers is a supply-side policy tool, since it operates on work incentives and effort. In question #1, the reduction in transfers is a fiscal policy tool, since it reduces consumer incomes and therefore their purchases.)

7. Draw the shift that will occur if the Federal Reserve decreases the money supply, thereby raising interest rates. What will be the effect on GDP and employment? _____ What will be the effect on the average price level? _____

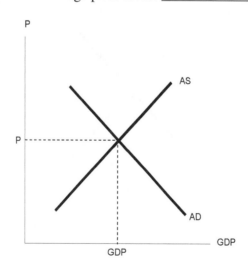

8. Draw the shift that will represent each of the following examples of inflation. In the blank provided, tell what type of inflation is occurring.

a. _____ The government decides to go to war with another country, and increases its purchases of armaments.

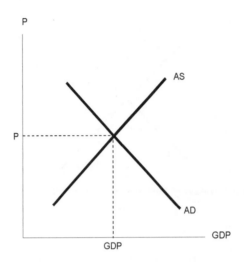

b. _____ Rising energy prices increase the costs of production of all businesses that use energy in their production process.

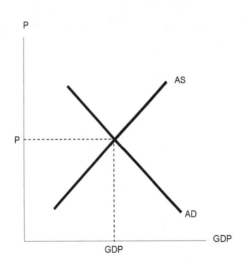

c. _____ Increased market power results in business decisions to restrict output in order to drive up prices.

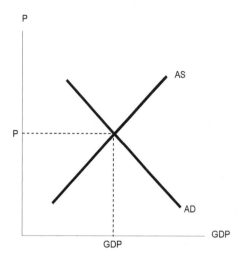

9. (Appendix) What is the effect of an increase in AD in the horizontal position of AS? _____ In the vertical position of AS? (Show your answers on the graph). _____

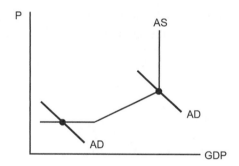

SELF-TEST

Multiple-Choice Questions

1. When referring to GDP in one particular year, we want to use:
   a. real GDP.
   b. nominal GDP.
   c. GDP calculated using constant prices (i.e. the prices of a base year).
   d. none of the above.

2. Gross domestic product (GDP) differs from gross national product (GNP) in that GDP:
    a. refers to production by the economy.
    b. refers to production in the economy.
    c. refers to production of goods only.
    d. refers to production of services only.

3. Underground activity:
    a. refers to the total production of services in our economy.
    b. refers to illegal activity and unreported economic activity.
    c. refers to agricultural production (crops produced under the ground).
    d. all of the above.

4. Which of the following is *not* represented by the aggregate demand curve?
    a. consumer purchases.
    b. business purchases.
    c. purchases of U.S. GDP by foreigners.
    d. purchases of foreign products by U.S. citizens.

5. Business purchases represented by aggregate demand include:
    a. purchases of factories.
    b. purchases of machinery.
    c. "purchases" of inventories.
    d. all of the above.

6. Which of the following is *not* correct? Government purchases of goods and services includes:
    a. government purchases of office supplies for public schools.
    b. government purchases of teacher services in public schools.
    c. government income transfers to private individuals.
    d. government purchases of the services of police officers.

7. Cost-push inflation is caused by:
    a. anything that increases aggregate demand.
    b. anything that increases costs of production.
    c. market power that increases profits.
    d. anything that pulls down aggregate demand.

8. Which of the following is a tool of *contractionary* fiscal policy?
    a. reduced taxes.
    b. increased transfers.
    c. increased regulations.
    d. decreased government purchases of goods and services.

9. Monetary policy is directly under the control of:
    a. the President.
    b. the Congress.
    c. the Federal Reserve.
    d. the mayors of major cities.

10. Which of the following can be a tool of (expansionary) supply-side policy?
    a. reduced tax rates.
    b. reduced transfers.
    c. reduced regulations.
    d. all of the above.

11. Which of the following is an income transfer?
    a. food stamps.
    b. Social Security cash benefits.
    c. housing assistance for the poor.
    d. all of the above.

12. Different fiscal policy tools will result in different:
    a. composition of GDP.
    b. roles for the government in the economy.
    c. roles for the private sector of the economy.
    d. all of the above.

13. Which of the following is *not* part of current GDP?
    a. purchases of theater tickets.
    b. purchases of hair cuts.
    c. purchases of a 10-year-old home.
    d. purchases of restaurant dinners.

14. Which of the following is *not* true? Expansionary monetary policy causes:
    a. increased interest rates
    b. increased GDP
    c. increased employment
    d. an increased average price level

15. (Appendix) The aggregate demand curve is downward sloping due to:
    a. the international trade effect of a change in the average price level
    b. the value of real wealth effect of a change in the average price level
    c. the interest rate effect of a change in the average price level
    d. all of the above

16. (Appendix) Expansionary fiscal policy in the context of the vertical portion of the aggregate supply curve results in:
    a. an increase in GDP.
    b. an increase in employment.
    c. an increase in the average price level.
    d. all of the above.

True-and-False Questions

1. Aggregate demand is defined as the quantity of total output (GDP) demanded (purchased) at alternative average price levels.

2. Gross domestic product is tabulated in terms of market prices.

3. Gross national product refers to goods and services produced *in* (that is, within the geographical boundaries of) the country.

4. When comparing GDP over several years, we want to use "nominal GDP."

5. Vegetables from your own garden that you consume directly are not counted as part of GDP.

6. Illegal drug trade is considered to be underground activity.

7. Consumer purchases are the largest component of GDP.

8. Business purchases are generally the most stable (non-fluctuating) component of GDP.

9. Unemployment compensation is an example of an income transfer.

10. Expansionary fiscal policy can include cuts in taxes.

11. GDP is expressed in terms of physical quantities, not dollar values.

12. Non-durable goods last for less than one year.

13. Trickle-down philosophy includes the notion that benefits of economic growth eventually benefit everyone.

14. Services such as hair cuts and health care are not part of GDP.

15. Business purchases represent the largest share of aggregate demand.

16. Stagflation is defined as simultaneous recession and inflation.

17. The "P" on the vertical axis of the graph of aggregate demand and aggregate supply refers to the average price level in the economy.

18. The production of a Canadian citizen living in the United States is a part of U.S. GDP.

19. The production of a U.S. citizen living in Canada is a part of the U.S. GDP.

20. The term "market price" refers to the price of a product before adding on any sales and excise taxes.

21. Aggregate supply refers to the quantity of total output supplied (produced) at alternate average price levels.

ANSWERS TO PRACTICE QUESTIONS

1. A decrease in government income transfers in this question will lower consumer incomes, which will reduce the consumer portion of aggregate demand. The decrease in AD results in a reduction in GDP, employment, and the average price level. (Remember: Always shift the curve first, then read the answers about GDP, employment, and the average price level off of the graph!!! Also remember that employment is linked to GDP. When GDP goes up, so does employment; when GDP goes down, so does employment.)

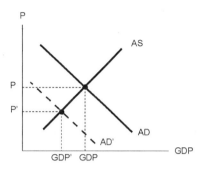

2. An increase in government purchases of police protection services will increase the government portion of aggregate demand. The increase in AD results in an increase in GDP, employment, and the average price level.

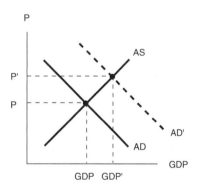

3. In increase in regulations will raise the costs of production, thereby reducing profit margins and incentives to produce, thereby reducing aggregate supply. This will cause a reduction in GDP and employment, and a rise in the average price level. (Always remember that a decrease in aggregate supply is a *backwards* shift of the curve!)

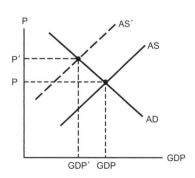

4. An increase in tax rates in this question will result in reduced incentives for work effort, and thereby a decrease in aggregate supply. This will cause a reduction in GDP and employment, and a rise in the average price level.

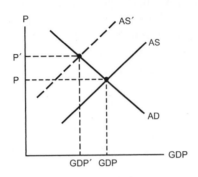

5. An increase in taxes in this question will decrease the after-tax income of consumers, resulting in a decrease in consumption purchases, and therefore a decrease in aggregate demand. This will result in a decrease in GDP, employment, and the average price level.

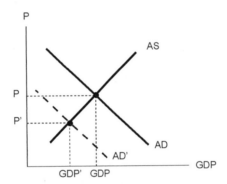

6. A reduction in transfers in this question will result in incentives for greater work effort, and therefore an increase in aggregate supply. This will cause an increase in GDP and employment, and a decrease in the average price level.

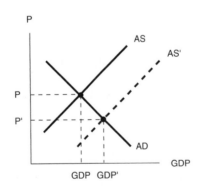

7. A decrease in the money supply will cause an increase in interest rates, which will reduce investment (purchases of factories, etc.). This implies a reduction in aggregate demand (since investment represents a portion of AD), which will cause a decrease in GDP, employment, and the average price level.

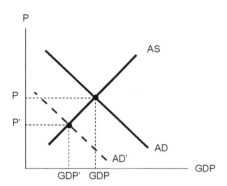

8. a. Increases in purchases of armaments represents an increase in aggregate demand, raising the average price level. This is called demand-pull inflation.

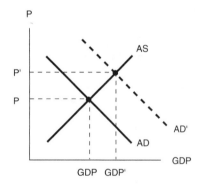

    b. Rising energy prices increase the costs of production, thereby decreasing aggregate supply and causing a rise in the average price level. This is called cost-pull inflation.

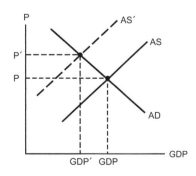

c.   Increased market power is used to restrict output and drive up prices, which represents a decrease in aggregate supply. This is called profit-push inflation.

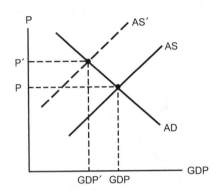

9.   (Appendix) An increase in GDP and employment and no change in the average price level; an increase in the average price level but no change in GDP and employment.

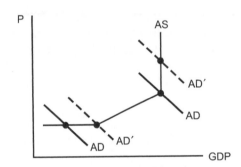

ANSWERS TO SELF-TEST

Multiple-Choice: 1b, 2b, 3b, 4d, 5d, 6c, 7b, 8d, 9c, 10d, 11b, 12d, 13c, 14a, 15d, 16c
True-and False: 1T, 2T, 3F, 4F, 5T, 6T, 7T, 8F, 9T, 10T, 11F, 12T, 13T, 14F, 15F, 16T, 17T, 18T, 19F, 20F, 21T

16

Taxes, Borrowing, and the National Debt

PURPOSE

Here we are at the last of our "stability" chapters. Everyone is interested in taxes, since we all end up paying them one way or another. And the issue of government borrowing is a front page news story with the recent tax cuts, war-related spending, and even space travel, that are eliminating the government budget surplus of just a few years ago! The purpose of this chapter is to introduce you to these concepts of taxes and government borrowing, as well as the national debt. The objective is to explain and clarify these concepts without being overly technical. This is one of those chapters that covers material that everyone (i.e. the public) knows a little about (as in "taxes are too high, and so is the national debt!"), but nobody (i.e. the public) really understands enough to see the whole picture. The concept of government borrowing is particularly confusing to the public, as is the distinction between the budget deficit and the national debt. After completing this chapter, you will find that you can easily understand what you thought to be difficult material, and you will have a much more informed perspective on these issues than the general public (not to mention the politicians!).

LEARNING OBJECTIVES

The learning objectives for this chapter are:

1. to acquaint you with our various types of taxes, including income, and social insurance, excise, sales, and property taxes.

2. to acquaint you with the basic operation of our income tax system, as well as the terms tax rate, tax base, exemption, standard deduction, and tax credit.

3. to enable you to understand the effects of taxes on the macro economy, income distribution, and individual markets.

4. to help you understand the distinction among taxes that are regressive, proportional, and progressive.

5. to assist you in understanding the process of government borrowing and its effects on the macro economy, income distribution, interest rates, and crowding out.

6. to help you understand the difference between budget deficits and the national debt, and the proper way to consider their size.

7. to enable you to understand the impact of the national debt and proposals that require a balanced budget, and to discover your own perspective (liberal or conservative) on these topics.

STUDY SUGGESTIONS

- As always, carefully read the definitions of the vocabulary words to be sure you understand the meaning of each term and can use it in a sentence.

- When studying the graphs of aggregate demand and aggregate supply, be sure to redraw these graphs on your own. This will help you understand the material, and you will be more likely to remember it for an exam. This should be your practice when studying any of the graphs in the text.

- The terms regressive, proportional, and progressive refer to tax payments as a *percentage of income*. Often high income people pay a much larger *amount* of tax dollars than low income people. This is not the issue, however, when we consider the concepts of regressivity versus progressivity. In other words, progressive taxes take a larger *percentage of income* from high income people than low income people, proportional taxes take the same *percentage of income* from people of all income levels, and regressive taxes take a larger *percentage of income* from low income people than high income people. Does it surprise you that so many of our taxes are regressive?

- Think about whether you would cut down smoking (if you smoke), cut down drinking (if you drink), and cut down driving (if you drive) if the government imposed a higher excise tax on cigarettes, alcohol, and gasoline, which would raise the prices of these products. One reason that excise taxes are imposed on these types of products is that people generally do not cut down very much on their consumption of these when prices rise (that is, their demand is inelastic). This means that government excise tax revenue will be higher on these types of products than those that people stop buying due to higher prices.

- Again, be sure you redraw the graph of the market for loanable funds. Don't let the concept of financial markets scare you! We are still just talking about demand and supply. Demand is the demand for loanable funds by all borrowers. Supply is the supply of loanable funds by all lenders and savers. The price of money, which is the interest rate, will increase or decrease as the demand for loanable funds increases or decreases.

- Don't be confused between the concepts of the budget deficit and the national debt! Many people use these terms interchangeably, without really knowing what they are saying. The budget deficit is an annual concept. It shows the difference between government spending and tax revenue in a particular year. On the other hand, the national debt represents all the money that the government has ever borrowed and not yet repaid. Clearly a budget deficit will increase the size of the national debt, while a budget surplus can reduce its size. These are not the same concepts however.

- Don't be confused between the concepts of the government budget deficit and the trade deficit! They are not the same! The trade deficit is the difference between imports and exports. The budget deficit is the difference between government spending and tax revenue. Both are annual concepts.

- Don't be confused between the concepts of the national debt and international debt! International debt is usually discussed in the context of the large debt that developing countries incurred during the 1970s and the 1980s. This developing country debt is owed to foreign governments and institutions, and is discussed in more detail in Chapter 17. The national debt of the United States is owed primarily to U.S. citizens and institutions. Even the relatively small share of the national debt that is owed to foreigners does not create the same problem of international debt faced by developing countries, since nations readily accept repayment in dollars but not in other non-convertible currency.

- Think about the capital Viewpoint section. Where do you stand?

Work through the practice exercises and take the self-test. Be certain you understand anything you miss.

PRACTICE EXERCISES

1. Show in the graphs the effects of the following. Which example results in a larger expansion of the economy? _____

   a. Increased government spending on national defense (of $1 million) financed by government borrowing (of $1 million).

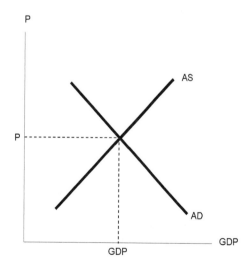

b. Increased government spending on national defense (of $1 million) financed by increased taxes (of $1 million).

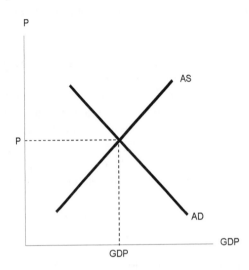

2. Calculate the effects of a sales tax on hypothetical higher and lower income families over one year, using the following data:

	Higher Income Family	Lower Income Family
Income	$400,000	$40,000
Purchases of taxable goods and services	$200,000	$36,000
Sales tax rate	10%	10%
Amount of sales tax paid	_____	_____
Amount of sales tax paid as a % of income	_____	_____

3. To examine why the Social Security tax is regressive, let's assume that you are a poor student and I am a filthy rich professor (NOT!). Let's assume that you earn $10,000 per year by working and I earn $50,000 through teaching, another $450,000 through consulting, another $500,000 in capital gains, $200,000 in interest income, and $300,000 in dividends. Your total income is $10,000 per year and mine is $1,500,000.

    a. First calculate the amount of Social Security tax that you must pay, recalling that you are taxed at the rate of 6.2% on all of your income (since it is all earned through working and it falls below the $76,000 income limit). What is the total amount you must pay? _____ What share of income must you pay? _____

b. Now calculate the Social Security taxes that I must pay. Note that the last three forms of my income (capital gains, interest income, and dividends) are not subject to the Social Security tax. Also note that my earnings from working are $500,000 ($50,000 + $450,000). However, only the first $76,000 of these earnings are subject to the Social Security tax rate. What is the total amount that I must pay? _____ What share of my income must I pay? (Remember to divide the total amount of tax I must pay by my entire income of $1,500,000.) _____

c. Do you now see how the Social Security tax is regressive? _____

4. Consider the hypothetical market for long distance phone service on the following graph. Draw the shift that will occur with the imposition of an excise tax. What is the effect on the price paid by consumers? _____ What is the effect on the quantity of long distance phone service? _____ Who bears the burden of the excise tax? _____ (Extra from the appendix: who bears the burden of the tax if the demand for long distance phone service is perfectly inelastic? _____)

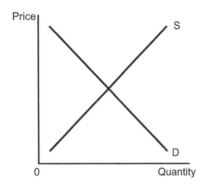

5. Shift the curve in the market for loanable funds that occurs when the government borrows money. What is the effect on interest rates? _____

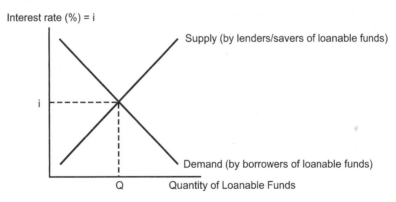

6. Government spending of $100 billion and tax revenue of $70 billion in a particular year results in a budget deficit of _____.

SELF-TEST

Multiple-Choice Questions

1. Which tax brings in the *second* greatest share of federal government tax revenue?
    a. federal personal income tax.
    b. social security tax.
    c. federal excise taxes.
    d. tariffs.

2. Until 1964, the federal income tax rate for very highest increments of income was about:
    a. 90%.
    b. 70%.
    c. 60%.
    d. 10%.

3. The capital gains tax is placed on:
    a. the amount of money a person receives when selling an asset.
    b. the difference between what a person receives when selling an asset and the price the person paid when buying the asset.
    c. the amount of money borrowed in order to purchase an asset.
    d. the difference between what a person borrows and later repays when purchasing an asset.

4. Which of the following brings in the largest share of combined state and local government tax revenue?
    a. sales and excise taxes.
    b. personal income taxes.
    c. corporate income taxes.
    d. property taxes.

5. An increase in personal income taxes will cause a decrease in:
    a. after-tax income.
    b. consumption spending.
    c. aggregate demand.
    d. all of the above.

6. Which of the following is *not* a regressive tax?
    a. sales tax.
    b. property tax.
    c. social security tax.
    d. federal personal income tax rate structure.

7. Which of the following is correct? A progressive tax:
    a. takes a larger amount of tax dollars from low income people than high income people.
    b. takes a larger percentage of income from low income people than high income people.
    c. takes a larger percentage of income from high income people than low income people.
    d. none of the above.

8. The total amount of money that the government has ever borrowed and has not yet repaid is:
    a. the budget deficit.
    b. the trade deficit.
    c. the national debt.
    d. crowding out.

9. Economists generally believe that a law or constitutional amendment requiring a balanced budget:
    a. is a good way to use fiscal policy.
    b. is a good way to use monetary policy.
    c. can be destabilizing for the economy.
    d. they have no opinion.

10. Approximately what share of the national debt is owned by (owed to) various levels and agencies of the government and federal reserve system?
    a. 1%.
    b. 16%.
    c. 56%.
    d. 81%.

11. President George W. Bush's tax proposals and policies would:
    a. reduce federal personal income tax rates.
    b. reduce or eliminate the estate tax.
    c. result in a less progressive (more regressive) tax system.
    d. all of the above.

12. An amount of money that can be taken off of a person's entire federal income tax bill is a:
    a. tax deduction.
    b. tax exemption.
    c. tax credit.
    d. tax base.

13. (Appendix) An excise tax placed on a product with a perfectly inelastic demand will place the burden of the tax:
    a. primarily on the consumer.
    b. entirely on the consumer.
    c. primarily on the supplier.
    d. entirely on the supplier.

True-and-False Questions

1. The government borrows money when it issues government securities.

2. A tax credit reduces the amount of personal income tax payable to the government.

3. Capital gains refer to the interest earned when someone has money in a savings account.

4. Property taxes are used to finance local public schools.

5. Increased government spending financed by increased taxes creates greater expansion of the economy than if the increased government spending is financed by government borrowing.

6. A regressive tax is one that takes a larger percentage of income from low income families than from high income families.

7. Property taxes are generally considered to be progressive.

8. An excise tax generally results in a higher price of the product, though the price generally does not increase by the full amount of the excise tax.

9. Increased government borrowing will generally cause a decrease in interest rates.

10. "Crowding out" refers to a situation whereby increased government borrowing results in increased interest rates, thereby causing some reduction in private borrowing.

11. The budget deficit is the difference between government spending and government tax revenue in any one year.

12. The national debt will eventually bankrupt our nation.

13. Government securities include government bonds and treasury bills

14. A "tax base" could be income, earnings, value of purchase, property, and so on.

15. Once fully phased in, President Bush's personal income tax cuts will result in a maximum tax rate of 85%.

16. The earned income credit is "refundable."

17. Excise taxes bring in a very small share of total federal tax revenue.

18. The sales tax is a regressive tax.

19. A regressive tax takes a larger dollar amount from low income people than high income people.

20. The largest share of combined state and local government tax revenue comes from state and local personal income taxes.

ANSWERS TO PRACTICE EXERCISES

1. Answer "a" shows the larger expansion of the economy (GDP).

    a. Increase aggregate demand, which causes an increase in GDP.

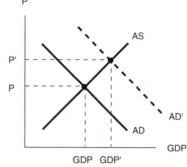

    b. Increase aggregate demand, but then decrease aggregate demand (but not quite back to the original aggregate demand curve). This is because an increase in taxes by $1 million reduces consumers' after-tax income by $1 million. This causes a reduction in consumer purchases by something less than the $1 million (since most people do not reduce spending by the full amount of an income decline.)

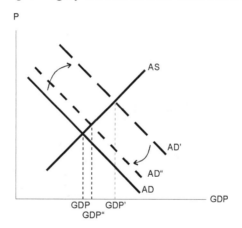

2. High income family: sales tax $= \$ 20,000$
    Sales tax as % of income $= \dfrac{\$ 20,000}{\$400,000} = .05 = 5\%$

    Low income family: sales tax $= \$ 3,600$
    Sales tax as % of income $= \dfrac{\$ 3,600}{\$ 40,000} = .09 = 9\%.$

3. Low income student:
    Social Security tax amount $= 0.062 \times \$10,000 = \$620$
    Social Security tax as a share of total income $= \$620 / \$10,000 = 6.2\%$

    High income professor:
    Social Security tax amount $= 0.062 \times \$76,000 = \$4,724.40$
    Social Security tax as a share of total income $= \$4,724.40 / \$1,500,000 = 0.3\%$

4. The excise tax is viewed as an increased cost of production, so it shifts the aggregate supply curve backwards (a decrease in supply). This will reduce the quantity, raise the price to consumers, and reduce the profits of the suppliers. Therefore, the burden is shared by both consumers and suppliers. (Extra from the appendix: if the demand for long distance service is perfectly inelastic, the price will go up by the full amount of the tax, and the full burden will be borne by consumers. Remember: the greater burden goes to the group with the more inelastic curve.)

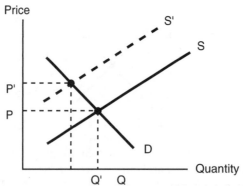

5. Increase in interest rates

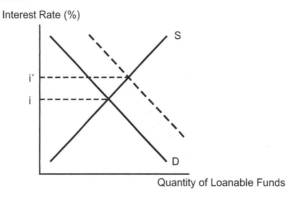

6. A budget deficit of $30 billion.

ANSWERS TO SELF-TEST

Multiple-Choice: 1b, 2a, 3b, 4d, 5d, 6d, 7c, 8c, 9c, 10c, 11d, 12c, 13b

True-and-False: 1T, 2T, 3F, 4T, 5F, 6T, 7F, 8T, 9F, 10T, 11T, 12F, 13T. 14T, 15F, 16T
17T, 18T, 19F, 20F

17

Globally Free Markets for the Twenty-First Century?

PURPOSE

The purpose of this final chapter in the book is to raise the question of whether the worldwide movement toward free markets will be successful. Success will hinge not only on economic growth variables, but on social indicators that reflect the standards of living of each country's residents. This chapter will enable you to synthesize all you have learned about liberal and conservative philosophy up until now, and to decide for yourself whether you favor a global shift towards freer markets or toward more government intervention in economies.

LEARNING OBJECTIVES

The learning objectives for this chapter are:

1. to contribute to your awareness of global conditions and issues.

2. to reinforce for you the entire textbook discussion of conservative versus liberal philosophies, this time in a truly global context.

3. to reinforce for you the difference between capitalism and socialism.

4. to help you understand the economic growth process in the Western industrialized world and policies designed to achieve growth.

5. to enable you to understand the most significant global economic phenomenon of the previous century; i.e. the economic transition that is still taking place in the formerly socialist industrialized world.

6. to help you understand the legacy of the international debt crisis, its impact on the standards of living of less developed country (LDC) residents, and its repercussions for LDC finances and subsequent economic reform.

7. to help you think about possible backlash to the global movement toward free markets.

8. to enable you to intelligently formulate your own opinions on the global movement toward free markets, and to determine whether your own economic philosophy is liberal, conservative, or in-between.

STUDY SUGGESTIONS

*   As always, be sure you understand the definitions of the vocabulary words.

*   Again, as always, reinforce your understanding of the graphs by redrawing the graphs of the macroeconomy and production possibilities and drawing any changes that occur in these graphs. Make sure you understand why these changes occur.

*   Realize that although we've applied them to three different regions of the world, the terms economic growth, transition to capitalism, and economic reform all represent a movement toward freer markets in the context we've used them here. They may have a positive, or negative, or mixed impact on the people of the regions.

*   By now you should have a pretty good understanding of the words liberal and conservative. You now have the opportunity to expand these concepts to the global economy, in terms of socialism versus capitalism. Remember that we are using the terms liberal and conservative in terms of *economic* philosophy and in U.S. terminology. For example, terms the liberal and liberalism have entirely different meanings.

*   By the end of this chapter and textbook, you've had the opportunity to decide for yourself whether you are liberal or conservative on economic topics. You are certainly welcome to be liberal on some and conservative on others!

*   By the end of this chapter and textbook, you will have had the opportunity to discover a little bit about the rest of the world, including the formerly socialist countries and the less developed countries. I hope this sparks your interest to study more about these countries, and even to travel some of them someday. I also hope you've decided that you'd like to use your education to make our world a better place. You've already begun the first step, which is becoming educated. For additional ideas about how you can achieve greater economic and social justice in our world, please be sure to read the Epilogue to this book. Thank you for your willingness to learn about the economics of social issues, and good luck to you with your life-long learning!

Work through the practice exercises and take the self-test. Make sure you understand any material you may have missed.

PRACTICE EXERCISES

1. Consider the graph of the macroeconomy. Draw the shift that will occur if cuts in tax rates and transfers successfully create incentives for greater work effort. What will be the effect on GDP? _____ What type of policy would we call this? _____

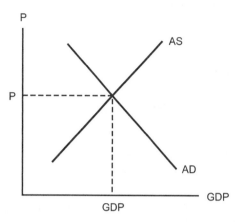

2. Consider the following graph of production possibilities, with consumer goods and capital goods on the two axes. Draw the effect of an improvement in the quality of the labor force. What do we call the result of this change? _____

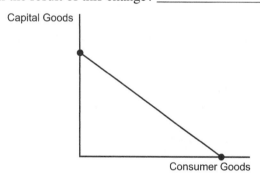

SELF-TEST

Multiple-Choice Questions

1. Which of the following is true? Conservatives believe that free markets:
    a. are efficient.
    b. provide incentives.
    c. encourage economic growth.
    d. all of the above.

2. In terms of the categories defined in the text, Russia belongs to:
    a. the Western industrialized world.
    b. the formerly socialist industrialized world.
    c. the less developed world.
    d. none of the above.

3. "Ways of using available resources to produce output" is the definition for:
    a. liberalism.
    b. economic growth.
    c. technology.
    d. conditionality.

4. Under capitalism, the means of production are owned by:
    a. the private sector.
    b. the public sector.
    c. the government.
    d. the Federal Reserve.

5. An improvement in technology results in:
    a. economic growth.
    b. decontrol of prices.
    c. economic reform.
    d. conditionality.

6. Decontrol of prices in the formerly socialist countries generally leads to:
    a. inflation.
    b. an elimination of shortages.
    c. higher prices.
    d. all of the above.

7. Which of the following is *not* true? Elements of economic reform generally include:
    a. decontrol of prices.
    b. privatization.
    c. reduction in government spending.
    d. increase of government involvement in the economy.

8. The oil price increases of the 1970s resulted in:
    a. the "recycling" of oil revenue.
    b. inflation.
    c. LDC borrowing from the International Monetary Fund.
    d. all of the above.

9. U.S. contractionary monetary policy of the early 1980s created:
    a. rising interest rates.
    b. recession.
    c. rising value of the dollar.
    d. all of the above.

10. "The international debt crisis" refers to:
    a. the U.S. national debt and its repercussions internationally.
    b. the problem that oil-producing countries have as they struggle to generate foreign exchange.
    c. the fact that less developed countries have had great difficulty repaying money they have borrowed from other countries and the IMF.
    d. the fact that the formerly socialist industrialized countries are privatizing government enterprises.

11. A decrease in government regulation:
    a. reduces business costs of production.
    b. may or may not shift the production possibilities curve outward, depending on its effect on the environment.
    c. is generally favored by economic conservatives.
    d. all of the above.

12. Which of the following Western industrialized countries had the highest average annual growth rate of GDP over the 1990s?
    a. Ireland.
    b. the U.S.
    c. Japan.
    d. Switzerland.

13. Policy proposals to increase the U.S. savings rate include which of the following?
    a. decrease in the capital gains tax.
    b. increase in tax breaks for various types of savings, such as IRAs.
    c. a consumption tax to replace the personal income tax.
    d. all of the above.

14. Which of the following events might create economic growth?
    a. increase in the savings rate.
    b. improvement in technology.
    c. increase in labor productivity.
    d. all of the above.

15. Labor productivity depends on:
    a. capital and technology used in the production process.
    b. human capital.
    c. training and education programs.
    d. all of the above.

True-and-False Questions

1. Liberals believe that the market place is always fair.

2. Under socialism, economic decisions are made by the public (government) sector.

3. Artificially low prices result in shortages.

4. Alternative combinations of output that a country can possibly produce are shown by the "technology possibilities curve."

5. A consumption tax is a tax on income that is saved (not consumed).

6. "Total savings divided by GDP" is the definition of capital gains.

7. The U.S. has the highest savings rate in the world.

8. Production possibilities assumes that resources are fully and efficiently used.

9. Privatization will eliminate all of the problems in Russian industry.

10. "Petrodollars" is the name given to dollars that go to capital flight.

11. A patent is a government grant of exclusive rights to use or sell a new technology or product for a period of time.

12. Capital flight occurs when people take money out of savings accounts and store it in their homes.

13. "Conditionality" is the obligation to meet certain requirements in exchange for financial assistance.

14. Russia has experienced a very high rate of growth of GDP over the 1990s.

15. Countries with socialist economic systems always have communist political systems.

16. The world as a whole is engaged in a transition from capitalism to socialism.

17. The current U.S. savings rate is about 50%.

18. Japan and the United States have the highest number of applications for patents in the world.

19. The average annual growth rates in the formerly socialist industrialized countries have all been positive over the 1990s.

ANSWERS TO PRACTICE EXERCISES

1. The AS curve shifts forward, GDP will increase. This is supply-side policy.

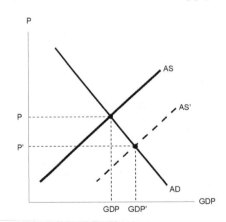

2. The production possibilities curve shifts outward, this is economic growth.

ANSWERS TO SELF-TEST

Multiple-Choice: 1d, 2b, 3c, 4a, 5a, 6d, 7d, 8d, 9d, 10c, 11d, 12a, 13d, 14d, 15d

True-and-False: 1F, 2T, 3T, 4F, 5F, 6F, 7F, 8T, 9F, 10F, 11T, 12F, 13T, 14F, 15F, 16F, 17F, 18T, 19F